TRICKSTER
MAGIC

TRADITIONAL

MODERN

DEITY

KIRSTEN RIDDLE

TRICKSTER MAGIC

TAP INTO THE ENERGY AND POWER
OF THESE IRRESISTIBLE RASCALS

HUMAN

ANIMAL

CICO BOOKS

LONDON NEW YORK

This book is dedicated to the Rev. Jeff Reynolds (July 22 1959–April 16 2014).
A mercurial and magnificent man, who embodied all the positive aspects
of the trickster; you are and always will be deeply missed.

Published in 2015 by CICO Books

An imprint of Ryland Peters & Small Ltd

20–21 Jockey's Fields   341 E 116th St
London WC1R 4BW   New York, NY 10029

www.rylandpeters.com

10 9 8 7 6 5 4 3 2 1

Text © Kirsten Riddle 2015
Design and photography © CICO Books 2015

A CIP catalog record for this book is available
from the Library of Congress and the British
Library.

ISBN: 978 1 78249 264 1

Printed in China

Editor: Rosie Lewis
Designer: Paul Tilby
Illustrator: Qian Wu

Commissioning editor: Kristine Pidkameny
Editor: Dawn Bates
Art director: Sally Powell
Head of production: Patricia Harrington
Publishing manager: Penny Craig
Publisher: Cindy Richards

CONTENTS

Introduction   6
Which Trickster are You?   8

CHAPTER ONE
Animal Tricksters   10

Coyote   14
Anansi the Spider   16
Brer Rabbit   18
Raven   20
Crow   22
Manabozho   24
Monkey   26
Reynard the Fox   28
Taking it further   30

CHAPTER TWO
Human Tricksters   32

Appalachian Jack   36
Robin Hood   38
Whiskey Jack   40
Bamapana   42
The Mannegishi   44
The Pied Piper   46
The Saci   48
Till Eulenspiegel   50
Wakdjunkaga   52
Taking it further   54

CHAPTER THREE
Deity Tricksters   56

Loki   60
Hermes   62
Pan   64
Lugh   66
Eris   68
Eshu   70

Nezha   72
Maui   74
Tezcatlipoca   76
Taking it further   78

CHAPTER FOUR
Traditional Tricksters   80

Jack   84
Puck   86
Gwydion   88
Aengus   90
Bigmouth   92
Hitar Petar   94
Kitsune   96
Mayan Hero Twins   98
Taking it further   100

CHAPTER FIVE
Modern Tricksters   102

Captain Jack Sparrow   106
Bugs Bunny   108
The Joker   110
The Pink Panther   112
Peter Pan   114
Doctor Who   116
Jack Frost   118
Willy Wonka   120
Taking it further   122

The Trick in the Tale   124

Index   126
Acknowledgments   128

INTRODUCTION

Tricksters have been around since the beginning of time. These irresistible rascals are the arrogant charmers you love to hate. They're the individuals who get under your skin, and who—despite their disruptive nature—always seem to fall on their feet. Take Captain Jack Sparrow from the *Pirates of the Caribbean* movies. He's an unknown quantity, a character who seems to have no moral compass, and is always up to his neck in trouble, yet he has the uncanny ability to get out of it just as fast and often help others in the process. In most cases he comes up smelling of roses. Almost cartoonesque in the way they operate, many modern tricksters leap from animations. Think Bugs Bunny or the enigmatic and super-slick Pink Panther, able to slide gracefully into and out of trouble.

The trickster archetype is larger than life and twice as ridiculous, but it's here to stay because it's an important part of our culture and psyche. We need it, not necessarily to show us the way, but to show us our options and the possible outcome of our behavior. Tricksters teach by example, and show that there is joy and spiritual wisdom to be found in any situation. They also show us that facing fear is not necessarily a bad thing and that change, however unexpected or uncomfortable, can lead to greatness and the ability to tap into true potential.

A mercurial character, this archetype is the curveball. It represents the moment when the ceiling comes crashing down on your world and you realize that life can't always be planned. The trickster represents the twists and turns of fate, and, like the Tower card in the tarot pack, its energy is in the unexpected, when everything becomes blurred and foundations crumble. This may sound scary, but it is also liberating working with this kind of medicine. The Native Americans have long understood the power of the trickster and how it works in mysterious ways. They built their spirituality on legends of the master trickster Raven and his mixing pot, which created the world and all the beings in it. They threw in the indomitable Crow, with his wily ways and cocky attitude, and to top it off they brought to life Coyote, one of the most famous and successful tricksters of all time, and a real scoundrel to boot. Their stories are littered with this archetype because they quickly understood and identified with its power. They knew that life, rather than being a straight line from A to B, is full of quirks and undulations. To explain the spontaneous nature of all things, they worked with the energy of the trickster to create a positive outlook, develop wisdom, and manifest the things they needed.

We can do the same. We can look at trickster characters from mythologies around the world, and uncover the deeper meanings. We can learn about ourselves and the environment through their antics. We can develop spiritually, emotionally, and physically, while creating a whole new set of adventures in our life. The trickster is easy for us to identify with because we all have a bit of this archetype within us. It's the inner child that longs to stop working and have some fun, the prankster that lurks beneath our straight face. We're human, we can't help but be a mix of contradictions, and so we can understand tricksters. They make mistakes, for which they often pay; they do bad things for a good reason, or good things when they're trying to be bad. There is no rhyme or reason to the way they act, and it's impossible to predict what will come next. The tricksters have little control over their behavior; they just go with the flow. Sometimes that's what we have to do, so even when we don't fully understand what drives them, we can empathize because we might do the same. Sometimes there is no explanation for why a person behaves in a certain way. We are individuals and we have the freedom to think and act as we like, although we often hide behind rules and regulations. The trickster shows us that we don't always have to limit ourselves, that we can take a risk, a leap of faith into the unknown.

This book is an introduction to the ways of the trickster. It will show you how to work with this kind of exuberant magic in order to improve any area of your life, from love through career, money and success, and health and well-being. Each chapter covers a different group of trickster characters, from animal folklore through tales of the gods, and from traditional tricksters through those that are still relevant today. You'll learn about the stories and associations, and how to work with each trickster in order to get the most out of your life. Each entry includes a ritual to help you connect with the trickster and a magical practice that you can carry out to enhance the power. These suggestions will get you started and provide a springboard for your own rituals. Trickster energy is all around, and although it's impossible to control, you can embrace this magic and channel it to create the future you want.

Whether you already know something about the trickster archetype or you're a complete beginner, it doesn't matter. You can dip into this book at any point, start with a group of tricksters that you're drawn to, or read it from beginning to end. You may feel drawn to a particular character or mythology already, in which case this is a good starting point for you to understand and work some trickster magic. But if you'd like a helping hand identifying with which group of tricksters you have an affinity, take the following quiz. It will point out the differences between each group, and show you how to tap into their energy.

WHICH TRICKSTER ARE YOU?

1) What kind of comedy do you like?

a) Bawdy jokes that push the boundaries
b) Scenarios that you can identify with
c) Quirky and imaginative sketches
d) Slapstick routines and general silliness
e) Cool, acerbic one-liners

2) Imagine you've recently lost your job through no fault of your own. How do you approach the future?

a) Treat it as an opportunity to have an adventure
b) Spend some time with friends and family and make the most of the time off
c) Embrace your destiny, knowing that something better is around the corner
d) Evaluate any lessons learned, and begin the search for something new
e) Who needs to work for someone else? I'm my own boss!

3) What's your favorite type of food?

a) Barbecue
b) Home-cooked dinners
c) Fine dining French-style
d) A diner
e) Any kind of takeout

4) If you were planning to seduce your ideal partner, what would you do?

a) Something crazy, such as arranging a skydive together
b) Treat him/her to a massage and spa day
c) Make a grand gesture, such as naming a star after him/her
d) Go on a treasure hunt with a picnic to finish
e) Be yourself, and watch your soon to be beloved swoon in your company!

5) A friend is looking for love. What advice do you give her?

a) Go with your instincts and make it known that you're attracted to someone through your body language
b) Be accessible and approachable, and always have a big smile
c) Enchant admirers with some flirty, meaningful stares
d) Make prospective partners laugh
e) Act super-cool and disinterested—make them do all the hard work!

6) What type of program/movie do you enjoy watching?

a) Natural-history documentaries
b) Comedies
c) Blockbuster fantasy epics
d) Adventure stories
e) Slick thrillers

7) Your soul mate would have which one of the following qualities:

a) An adventurous streak
b) Warmth and understanding
c) A clever, inventive mind
d) A sense of humor
e) Style and finesse

8) A friend has betrayed you. What do you do?

a) Outsmart him/her in front of others
b) Let out your anger privately and then forgive
c) Plan a complicated revenge, if only in your head
d) Prove that you're a better person by being ultra-successful
e) Relax and act as though you're not bothered

9) Your best quality is your:

a) Wild side
b) Empathy
c) Charm
d) Ability to forgive
e) Wit

10) Which animal would you have as your totem?

a) A lion
b) A horse
c) A dragon
d) A wolf
e) A cat

Mostly As: Animal

If you scored mostly As, then you have an affinity with animal tricksters. Like them, you have a wild side. You enjoy pushing the boundaries and being spontaneous. Your adventurous attitude means that you often find yourself in tricky situations, but it also means you've lots of entertaining tales to tell. A natural performer, you enjoy taking center stage just like these tricksters. You're a storyteller, so you have the power to win people over. There's a part of you that wants to be loved and admired, and that often means you'll go out of your way to impress. Animal tricksters embrace their feral side. They know it's important to let go and have fun. Work with these wild characters to channel your exuberant energy and unleash your innate creativity on the world!

Mostly Bs: Human

If you chose mostly Bs, then you're drawn to human tricksters. You can identify with these characters and their escapades, and, like them, you have a vulnerable side. You seek approval from those around you, which makes you very agreeable and open. There's a warm, sunny side to your personality, but you can often appear naive. Others often underestimate you; they fail to realize how determined and tenacious you can be. You're a force to be reckoned with, just like the human tricksters in this book, and like them, you have a deep well of courage inside. When pushed into a corner, you're not afraid to face your fears. Tap into the human tricksters' magic, embrace the dark side, and use their considerable power to help you move forward with confidence into a bright new future!

Mostly Cs: Deity

If you scored mostly Cs, then the trickster deities are calling to you. Like them, you have a fatalistic attitude to life. You enjoy the unpredictable nature of destiny. Powerful and commanding, you're a natural leader and enjoy taking charge when circumstances allow. Like the deities that fall into this category, you can be both charming and manipulative. You know and understand how people work, and this empathy means that you can connect easily with others. Ambitious and hardworking, you enjoy a good challenge. Anything that gets your mind ticking over makes you smile, so you actively seek tricky situations in order to stretch yourself. Working with trickster deities will help you make the most of your communication skills, while learning how to overcome obstacles and attain the success you desire!

Mostly Ds: Traditional

Mostly Ds means that you're connected to the traditional tricksters who crop up in folk- and fairy tales. You identify with their youthful exuberance, and their ability to laugh at themselves. You have a good sense of humor and tend to take most things in your stride. Like those traditional tricksters, you accept your faults, and realize that there's much to learn in life. You're not afraid to have fun and embrace your inner child, and your playful nature can mean that you ruffle a few feathers along the way. You see life as a journey with lots of twists and turns, and your "come what may" attitude often irritates others who aren't as relaxed in their approach. Work with traditional tricksters to increase your wisdom and self-esteem, and to achieve the happy ending to your personal story!

Mostly Es: Modern

If you chose mostly Es, then you have an affinity with modern trickster characters. Like these sassy boys and girls, you're super-smooth and hard to pin down. You like to have an air of mystery about you, and prefer to keep others guessing about your motives. Enigmatic and alluring, you have many admirers, and this is partly down to your ability to remain cool and collected in a crisis, something you have in common with your trickster counterparts. The truth is that you feel fear like everyone else, but you're good at putting on a show and creating an air of confidence. Like the tricksters of today, your power comes from your self-belief and devil-may-care attitude, but this can also make you appear arrogant at times. Tap into the magic of modern tricksters to help you embrace the ebb and flow of life, and to develop an open heart.

10

CHAPTER ONE

Animal
Tricksters

Humans and animals are bound together in a dance upon this Earth. From prehistoric times to the present, we have always been fascinated with the creatures that share our world, so much so that many mythologies use animals as the base for their teachings. It's easy to see how and why this has happened, since certain types of animal display specific characteristics that are easily recognizable. Think of the mighty lion, glorious and proud, with its golden mane and fearsome roar; it exudes strength and confidence and is a natural leader. Then there is the timid, wide-eyed deer, always running, always fearful, but graceful in the way it navigates the landscape. We humanize animals and use tales and folklore to explain their behavior; we watch them in awe and sometimes fear; but most of all we long to communicate with them. That is why so many cultures include an aspect of shape-shifting in their sacred practices. It's a way of connecting with these animals and learning about their true nature. It makes sense, then, that the trickster archetype, which is so important to the human psyche, lends itself to their form. We associate certain attributes with the trickster and recognize the same attributes in different animals, making it easy to create magical tales and memorable characters that we can identify with.

Those of us who are drawn to animal tricksters know the power of nature and have an affinity with the environment. We celebrate wildlife and understand the uniqueness of every species. Of course, animal tricksters come in many forms, from the deeply powerful and unpredictable Raven of Native American folklore, to the outlandishly rude and manipulative Anansi, the spider of African tales. These tricksters have much to offer us. Their tales are enjoyable and enchanting, but also bold and cruel in the way nature often is. There is no glossing over the hard facts: animals kill and are killed. They hunt and they survive, and some become victims, but that is the natural order of things. To get the most out of animal tricksters you need to imagine walking in their skin. Imagine taking on their characteristics and see things through different eyes. Animal tricksters can make us question the way we see the world and change our perceptions. They turn up in our lives in many different guises, from recurring images to a natural urge to get to know more about a creature. We can identify with them while remaining objective, because the fact is we're not a coyote or a rabbit, we're human. They encourage us to use our imagination and have fun, to unleash our primal nature and take a walk on the wild side!

COYOTE

Coyote is one of the most popular and complicated of all the trickster characters. In some Native American myths he's a sacred being with the power of creation. It is thought that with a handful of mud he made all the people, and that he gave names to the animals. In other tales he's the scoundrel, the ultimate trickster, bawdy, greedy, and out for himself. An adventurer with some of the fool about him, Coyote steps into precarious situations without a second thought. Unsurprisingly, he often comes to a sticky end, but being highly powerful he has the ability to be reborn and live another day. Sometimes it seems that his trickster nature is governed by a need to do good. When the frog people claim all the water in the land for themselves, for example, Coyote steps in and takes some for the other species, because it's only fair. But this wisdom is often short-lived. In other tales, we see a gullible side to Coyote. Some tribes tell of how Coyote challenges the wind to a race. If Coyote wins, then the weather will remain dry and sunny in winter, but if the wind beats him, then it will be a windy, rainy season. Coyote soon speeds ahead, but the wind knows what a greedy soul he is, and so casts a spell to make the crops grow. When Coyote sees all the fresh vegetables around him, his hunger takes over and he starts to eat, giving the wind plenty of time to catch up and beat him. That is why it is always cold and windy in winter.

ASSOCIATIONS

Element ALL ELEMENTS (EARTH/AIR/FIRE/WATER)
General *Stars, pipe, smoke, the Fool tarot card*
Stone Amber/turquoise

RITUAL

According to Navajo legend, Coyote scattered the stars in the sky by stealing the crystals from the Black Sky God. Tap into Coyote's magic and attract exciting opportunities and adventures into your life. Gather a handful of small stones from your yard or local park. At night, stand beneath the stars and hold the stones in both hands. Say, "I embrace my rightful destiny. I'm a magnet for opportunity. I attract new adventures every day. By Coyote's spirit, I live and play!" Slowly spin around and scatter the stones in every direction. Imagine you're scattering stars in the sky. When you've finished, spend a few minutes standing beneath the stars and imagine that each one is a personal wish or desire. Imagine reaching up into the sky and plucking the star. Say, "I claim my prize. I embrace my destiny every day!"

TEACHING

Be creative and adventurous, and embrace the ebb and flow of life. Be spontaneous, take a leap of faith, and—most importantly—trust your intuition.

MAGICAL PRACTICE

Howl like Coyote and unleash the magic of your creative spirit. Stand with your feet hip-width apart and your shoulders relaxed. Take a deep breath in and imagine a stream of energy running up from the ground and shooting through your body. As you breathe out, let your creative spirit flow and howl as loudly as you can, releasing any pent-up emotions!

TRICKSTER TIPS

Keep one of the stones you've collected as a memento of the ritual and a magical charm to attract new opportunities into your life. Carry it with you every day, and hold it while repeating the affirmation above.

ANANSI the SPIDER

Anansi is the West African deity who often takes the shape of a spider. He's a spinner of tales, a master storyteller, and is thought to be responsible for bringing stories to the Earth. He first appeared in Ghana, in the tales of the Ashanti and Akan peoples. These stories soon spread through west Africa and then eventually to the rest of the world. Like most tricksters, Anansi is cunning. He's rude and selfish, but also quick to learn. In one story he asks God for a new wife with no mouth on her face, because the old one is eating all his food (greed is another of Anansi's attributes). God provides him with a new wife with no mouth on her face, but the food still goes missing. Anansi realizes that this is because God tricked him and gave him a wife with a mouth in her armpit instead! He repents and begs forgiveness. He also promises not to be so selfish with his food, and although he does change, he doesn't lose all his selfish ways. In many tales Anansi acts as a messenger, helping humans to communicate their needs to the sky god Nyame, but usually he has an ulterior motive. Despite this, he is credited with giving both rain and night to the Earth. Although Anansi is manipulative, he redeems himself by showing that regardless of size it is possible to overcome any obstacle.

Anansi stories became so popular in Africa that they were renamed "spider tales." People soon realized that stories were a way of connecting with one another and manifesting miracles. Tap into Anansi's magic by using the oral tradition to create a positive future. Make up a narrative every morning. When you wake up, spend a few minutes telling the story of your day as you'd like it to be. Speak out loud and keep it simple and positive. For example, "Today I have an enjoyable journey into work. I arrive on time. I see my boss and impress her. I work well with my colleagues.
I get a fantastic promotion, which I celebrate with my family when I get home by enjoying a lovely meal.
I am happy and loved and today is a successful day." Speak in the present tense and imagine all the emotions you'll feel as each thing happens. Finish by saying, "I create the story of my life right now!" Do this every day for a month, and you'll notice fantastic opportunities and magical surprises falling into your lap!

MAGICAL PRACTICE

Improve your relationships with others by picturing threads like a spider's web stretching from your heart chakra in the center of your chest, connecting you to friends and family. See the web glisten with light, sending positive energy to your loved ones.

TEACHING

Use the power of words and the narratives you tell yourself and others to enhance your world magically and change your life for the better.

TRICKSTER TIPS

You can use the same technique to solve problems. If you find yourself in a tricky situation, just tell the story of how you'd like things to work out, making sure you conjure up the related emotions and a positive ending. Do this as many times as you like, and try out different scenarios and solutions until you find one that feels right.

ASSOCIATIONS

Element AIR/EARTH
General *Webs, circles, dew, the number 8*
Stone Quartz

BRER RABBIT

A lovable rascal, Brer Rabbit appears in African American folktales. He's the ultimate trickster character, quick-witted, mischievous, and cunning to the core. He is able to outrun and outsmart much bigger, stronger animals through his ingenuity. In most tales Brer Rabbit is matched by Brer Fox, or Brer Bear, but he always manages to beat them despite the dire nature of his circumstances. In the late 1800s author Joel Chandler Harris made Brer Rabbit tales popular with children and adults alike by creating a set of stories called the Uncle Remus tales. One of the most famous tales is the story of how Brer Fox tries to catch Brer Rabbit by using a tar baby. The rabbit gets stuck to the tar baby but instead of giving in, he tricks Brer Fox into throwing him into a briar bush. In most cases this would be a horrible and painful punishment for any creature, but Brer Rabbit has spent most of his life living in briar bushes, so he knows that he'll be able to wriggle free and escape. In another tale, he tricks Sis Cow into giving up her milk by trapping her horns in the bark of a tree. His quick-thinking charm is enough to make Sis Cow want to help him, and he's able to turn the situation to his advantage.

RITUAL

Try this ritual when you want to engage your imagination and attract more fun into your life. This is best carried out when the moon is full. Find a patch of soil outside, or if you prefer to stay inside, fill a washing-up bowl with soil, and stand barefoot in the earth. Breathe deeply and stretch your arms upward in a circular motion above your head, bringing them back down to your sides. Imagine your feet are rooted to the earth and that your head is being lightly tugged toward the sky. Feel the stretch of your spine as you stand tall and supported. Say, "Brer Rabbit, forager of the field, creature of the earth. Bless me with your wit and flair, shower me with mirth. Open up my mind and open up my heart. Unleash my creative spirit, let the adventure start!" Spend a few minutes enjoying the sensation of the soil between your toes. When you're ready, clean your feet and sprinkle the soil outside, repeating the chant above.

TRICKSTER TIPS

Rabbits are always on their toes and ready for action. Remember to flex your toes and spring gently up and down while carrying out this ritual. It will increase your physical and emotional flexibility.

MAGICAL PRACTICE

Carry a piece of moonstone in your pocket at all times for emotional healing, and to help you connect to the creative spirit of Brer Rabbit! Hold it in your left hand when seeking insights and solutions to problems.

TEACHING

Think laterally. Be flexible and adapt to any situation. It doesn't matter how helpless we may feel, there are always options if we can tap into our creative spirit!

ASSOCIATIONS

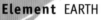

Element EARTH
General *Soil, brambles, bushes, the moon*
Stone Moonstone

BRER RABBIT

19

ANIMAL TRICKSTERS

In Native American mythology, Raven is not only a trickster but also the creator of all things. Although stories vary from tribe to tribe, it's commonly agreed that Raven brought light to the Earth. The tribes of the Pacific Northwest Coast also believe that he brought humans to Earth by releasing them from a cockle shell. Due to this, Raven is revered. His magic concerns the cycles of life and death, and many Native American people see him as the ultimate creator god. Despite this, it's common knowledge that Raven is a wily character who thinks only of himself. He brings mischief and mayhem to his dealings with humans. Raven is credited with creating the stars and the moon, a result of dropping some of the light he stole and scattering it through the sky. In one variant of the creation story, Raven started out completely white, but as he traveled with the sun the resulting smoke caught his feathers, turning him as black as the night. A master thief, Raven can and does steal anything that will

RAVEN

make his world a better place. Any benefit to humankind is usually by chance. Despite this, he is thought of as knowledgeable, having been taught everything about everything from his father. It was his father, a god of sorts, who gave Raven the power to create the world.

TEACHING

Remember that in the cycle of life, nothing stays the same. Shine your light at all times and be proud of who you are.

RITUAL

Embrace change by invoking the power of Raven. Take a dark-colored bowl, half-fill it with warm water, and add a couple drops of lavender essential oil. Place a piece of obsidian in the bowl. Next, light a black candle to represent the light that Raven stole, and the enlightenment that he brings humankind. Close your eyes and ask Raven to imbue you with his magic and wisdom. Ask him to show you an area in your life that needs change, or to bless you with an insight for the future. As you open your eyes, let your gaze fall into the watery depths. Thoughts, emotions, or images may pass through your mind; let them. You may even see shapes or patterns form on the water's surface. Don't force images or ideas, just let them flow into your mind. Spend a few minutes breathing deeply and enjoying the peace of your thoughts. As the candle burns down, take a notebook and write down any thoughts or feelings that stand out from your meditation—they could be insights that will help you in the future.

21

TRICKSTER TIPS

Repeat this ritual at the same time every week, preferably in the evening, and keep a log of any insights or revelations, as they may shed light on future issues. If you're seeking a vision in relation to a specific area, such as love or your career, carve the word relating to it into the wax of the candle.

MAGICAL PRACTICE

To energize your aura (the energy field around the body) and increase personal magnetism, take a black feather to represent Raven and flick it from head to toe, as if dusting your aura. Imagine two giant black wings extending outward, and then enveloping your body.

ASSOCIATIONS

Element AIR
General *The sun, the moon and stars, shells, bowls*
Stone Obsidian

Although not as prominent as Raven or Coyote, Crow is another trickster character in Native American mythology. He also appears in Australian Aboriginal folklore as one of the

CROW

main tricksters and a deeply respected ancestral being. Known for his cunning and dexterity, Crow has the ability to get what he wants, when he wants, often by kicking up a fuss. In the Kulin nation, in central Victoria, Crow features in many stories. He is thought to have brought fire to Earth and to have the ability to commune with the spirits. According to legend, the Karatgurk women (seven sisters who represented the Pleiades star cluster) guarded the Dreamtime fire and would not give up its secret to anyone. They carried burning coals on the end of their digging sticks. When Crow realized the power of the burning coals and how delicious it made his food taste, he tricked the women by burying a bundle of snakes in an anthill. He told them that these wriggling creatures were the ant's larvae and that they were far tastier than the yams they were used to eating. The sisters began digging the mound, angering the snakes, who attacked them. The women hit the snakes with their digging sticks, causing the coals to leap into the air. Crow cleverly caught the coals and stole them away. Although he did not at first want to share his find, eventually he threw some coals down to Earth. This caused a bush fire, which turned Crow's feathers as black as the coals he carried.

TEACHING

Speak up for what you believe in, express your truth, and communicate your needs to manifest your desires.

RITUAL

Find your true voice and tap into your higher self with this ritual. Take a black candle to represent Crow, light it, and spend a few minutes gazing into the flame. Now imagine a flame situated just above your navel and below your breastbone, in the area of the solar plexus. Feel it grow in size until it fills your chest with warmth. Imagine it stretching upward along your spine and neck and into your head. Feel the light behind your eyes illuminating your deepest thoughts and desires. Now imagine the flame bursting in a stream of fire from the top of your head and stretching upward into the universe. This flame connects you with the universal energy and fires your subconscious mind. Ask Crow to bless you with visions or insights that will help you on your future path. When you're ready, imagine the flame flickering and dwindling in size, until it remains a constant warmth in your chest, giving you the energy and determination to succeed.

MAGICAL PRACTICE

To communicate with a lost loved one, take a picture or a memento that reminds you of him/her, and place a black feather on top of it. Close your eyes and ask Crow to help you send a message of love. Visualize your loved one in front of you, and speak your message out loud. Your loved one may return the favor with a personal message, or just a feeling of love that sweeps over you.

TRICKSTER TIPS

Re-create the flame in your mind whenever you need a confidence boost, or to find the right words, for example in an interview or when you're trying to deal with an awkward situation. Imagine it burning bright, sending a powerful surge of Crow magic through your system!

ASSOCIATIONS

Element FIRE/AIR
General *Flames, candles, black feathers, silver coins*
Stone Smoky quartz/carnelian

This Algonquin trickster deity is also known as the Big Rabbit or Hare, and features in the tales of the Ojibway and Menominee people. A wheeler-dealer, Manabozho was known for his shape-shifting skills, transforming at the drop of a hat into a rabbit in order to flee trouble. With the powers of creation at his fingertips, Manabozho would sometimes appear as a human carrying a medicine bag, and it was thought that he brought the power and knowledge of medicine to the people. It was said that he was conceived when his father, the north wind, lifted up the skirt of a young girl with a gust of lusty air, and the result was this wayward offspring. Manabozho is famous for slaying monsters and for giving certain creatures their telltale characteristics and traits. Clever and wise but also reckless at times, Manabozho is a cultural hero and, like most of his trickster counterparts, makes mistakes that can benefit or hinder. A master of subterfuge, he once tricked a lone moose into believing he was its long-lost brother, lulling it into a false sense of security in order to kill and eat it.

MANABOZHO

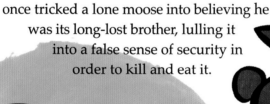

TEACHING

Face up to past mistakes and learn to forgive yourself and others in order to be healed and rejuvenated and improve your general well-being.

RITUAL

This energizing ritual will help you fire on all cylinders. Sage is a popular herb in Native American rituals, and it's also known for its medicinal properties, being anti-inflammatory. Take a bundle of freshly chopped sage and steep it in a cup of hot water. As the steam rises from the cup, use your hand or, if you prefer, a feather, to waft the vapor around your body, starting at the top of your head and working up and down both sides. As you do this, imagine you're spring-cleaning your aura. See it getting brighter and bigger until it extends outward like a thick layer of white light. Imagine any negative energy disintegrating as the bright, rejuvenating energy takes over. Say, "Manabozho, with your healing power, cleanse my body, mind, and soul. Strengthen my intellect and my charm, help me achieve any goal!" Breathe deeply and continue to inhale the aroma of sage until you feel relaxed and recharged.

MAGICAL PRACTICE

Tap into Manabozho's magic by including images of rabbits and hares around your home on pillows, pictures, or ornaments. The moon is also closely associated with the rabbit, so choose images of moon-gazing hares and wear jewelry in the shape of the moon.

TRICKSTER TIPS

If you prefer, drink an infusion of sage, being careful to remove the steeped leaves. As you sip the brew, picture your aura brightening. Repeat the magical affirmation above in your mind. This is particularly effective if you're suffering from a bad throat or a head cold, as the healing concoction clears the mind.

ASSOCIATIONS

Element AIR
General *Rabbits, hares, moon, wind, storms, herbs and medicines*
Stone Moonstone

MONKEY

This Chinese trickster was also a deity called Sun Wukong, known for his vanity and frivolous nature. This trickster tends to make mistakes at first, falling prey to foolish behavior and then learning from his error to save the day. Known as the "great sage equal to heaven," his wisdom lies in his ability to learn and move forward. Monkey is mischievous, a pleasure-seeker who can appear reckless at times. Fearing death, the Monkey King sought the secret of immortality. He consulted a Taoist sage, who gave him many gifts, one of which was the secret of "cloud flying." This meant that the Monkey King could summon a cloud to fly anywhere in the world. He also obtained a magical wishing staff from the Dragon King, which could grow to the size of the universe or shrink to the size of a pin. This came in handy when Monkey King was faced with demons and monsters. Like the Norse mythological character Loki, Monkey didn't just reserve his pranks for mortals; he also liked to play tricks on the other gods. As a result he was summoned to Heaven to be disciplined, but instead he wreaked havoc by eating the peaches of immortality. Ultimately, Buddha stepped in and tricked Monkey with a challenge to jump off the palm of his hand. Monkey agreed, but soon realized that he was trapped in the Buddha's hand. As punishment for his crimes, Monkey was buried beneath a mountain for many years, during which he repented and learned the art of patience.

TEACHING

It's never too late to show humility and learn from past mistakes, or to reinvent any aspect of yourself.

RITUAL

The Monkey King ate the peaches of immortality in an attempt to cause heavenly chaos, but equally the peaches would have given him much-needed wisdom and an insight into the future. The following ritual takes inspiration from this tale and from Monkey's ability to learn. Light a candle, then take a knife and cut a peach in half. The first half represents your past. As you eat this piece, think for a moment about all the things you've done, good and bad. Evaluate your life and be honest with yourself. When you've finished, say, "The past is gone, I move on." The second piece relates to the future. As you eat this piece, think about all the things you'd like to achieve. Picture them in your mind and imagine how you'll feel when you succeed in your dreams. Make the image and the emotions as vivid as you can. When you've finished eating this piece, say, "As I see, so it shall be."

MAGICAL PRACTICE

Release the past and reinvent yourself by finding a high spot of ground, such as a hill or mountain. Stand on the summit and in a loud voice shout the name of the thing you'd like to let go of. Breathe deeply, throw your arms open, and invite Monkey to bless you with wisdom and help you on a new path.

TRICKSTER TIPS

Peach-scented oil can be burned around the home to promote a happy, peaceful atmosphere and also to raise self-esteem. As you burn it, ask Monkey to bring joy and fun into your life.

ASSOCIATIONS

Element AIR
General *Clouds, flying, mountains, magical staff, peaches*
Stone Sunstone

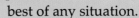

This trickster character features in tales from medieval Europe. A quirky chancer, Reynard crops up

REYNARD the FOX

in French folklore, where he assumes the mantle of the peasant hero, standing up for himself against the aristocracy. Considered to be a studious character, Reynard constantly outwits his opponents, seeking revenge on those who have done him wrong. In one famous tale, all the other animals (including Reynard's wife) believe him to be dead. At the funeral they gather and deliver insincere eulogies, not realizing that Reynard is hiding and can hear their words. He then hatches a cunning plan to get his own back on each one of them, including his own wife, who remarries shortly after his supposed death. A charismatic trickster, Reynard was a fast talker and, like his animal counterparts, knew how to make the best of any situation.

TRICKSTER TIPS

When you feel vulnerable or under attack, visualize a golden cloak of protection draped around your shoulders, a bit like the golden dome that covers your home in the ritual. Feel the warmth of the cloak shielding you from harm and infusing you with energy!

TEACHING

Be resourceful and flexible, adapt to the highs and lows of life, and always look for the positive in every situation. Look on the bright side and think on your feet to find a quick solution to a problem.

RITUAL

In European folk tales, Reynard lives in an impenetrable castle, where he always seeks refuge and gains strength. Take inspiration from this and make your own home your castle and seat of power. Place a small red votive in every room and light them all. Take a handful of earth, preferably from your yard, and mix it with a teaspoon of salt for protection. Sprinkle the mixture along the perimeter of your property. Finally, stand near your front door and imagine a cloak of golden light coming down from the sky and covering your home. This cloak of light provides a protective layer like a dome, keeping harmful energy at bay. Say, "In this sacred place my power grows, I'm strong and protected, my energy glows." Let the votives burn down. Repeat the ritual once a month to keep your home cleansed and maintain the positive energy you've created.

MAGICAL PRACTICE

Red is the color associated with Reynard the Fox, and it's also the color of action, passion, and energy. Revitalize your world by introducing this vibrant color into every area of your life. Wear splashes of red in your accessories and include it in your home by choosing soft furnishings, such as pillows, throws, and rugs, in various shades of russet. Think about your yard, too, and go for flowers and plants in bright and deep reds.

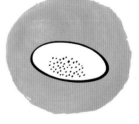

ASSOCIATIONS

Element EARTH
General *Red cloaks, flags, castles*
Stone Amber

Taking It Further

Animal tricksters come in many shapes and forms, but they're always a delight to discover. If you want to take your explorations further and work with animal trickster energy, try these top magical tips.

Get out and about and observe. Look at the wildlife around you. Get up close and personal and don't forget the little creatures, such as birds and insects. A creature doesn't have to be large in stature to contain powerful trickster magic. Take a notebook with you and write down your observations. If you feel inspired, make up stories about the animals you see and let the trickster come forward naturally in the narrative.

Take an animal trickster that already exists and give it a new story. Be creative and have fun. For example, you might decide to set the story in the present day, or you might place it in your own environment and include yourself in the narrative. Let your imagination take over!

Decorate your home with images of the trickster to which you feel most drawn. For example, if you feel a kinship with Brer Fox from the Brer Rabbit tales, then include images of foxes in their natural habitat around your home. You might include pictures or wallpaper with a foxy theme, or you might opt for fox-themed pillows, throws, drapes, and tablecloths. Think of the fox's natural coloring and use it in your decor to give you an energy boost. Also consider your own appearance, and choose jewelry and clothing that incorporate fox images and colors.

CHAPTER TWO

Human

Tricksters

We tend to think of tricksters as ethereal and mystical, as spiritual beings with magical powers who leap from the pages of a book, or are spoken about in whispers and by candlelight. Deities and shape-shifters, they are supernatural in their ability to control the elements, cause chaos, and be reborn any number of times. But they're also human, like us. Their ability to err, to misjudge, and to act spontaneously is something with which we can all identify. A Jungian archetype, the trickster lives within us. He's the fool stepping off the cliff, about to embark on a new adventure. He's the joker who lurks inside our head, providing us with the wit and humor to handle any situation. He's our inner child, waiting to be unleashed upon the world. Most of all, he's the survivor who drives us onward when we're faced with a seemingly insurmountable challenge. All these things mean that the trickster is actually more human than we might at first imagine. His core qualities are attributes that we know and recognize in ourselves, but he still manages to live both in this world and out of it, crossing the boundaries with his behavior wherever possible. The human trickster challenges authority, and pokes fun at those who take themselves too seriously.

In a way, the trickster represents the rebel in us all. Our ancestors recognized this and put it to good use, creating tales that have been passed down over the centuries. These stories were inhabited by outlandish heroes who defied the odds and used all manner of trickery to achieve their aims. They were real people who found themselves in precarious situations, sometimes because of their own actions, and sometimes because they were in the wrong place at the wrong time. These folk tales became a

blueprint for modern living. They showed us how to behave and pointed out the consequences of our actions, and they also gave us guidelines on what to do in certain situations. Those guidelines are still appropriate today. Many fairy tales started out as folk tales, which became more convoluted as time passed. These stories were often developed as a way of showing people how to deal with potential threats, which is why there is always an element of danger (the deep dark forest, the big bad wolf, the evil queen). The characters in these tales might not be obvious trickster types, but they have to take on some of those traits to survive. Often they find themselves thinking on their feet, standing up to authority, and taking huge risks in order to save the day—not unlike Coyote, or Loki, or any number of mystical trickster beings. Think about Hansel and Gretel, who find themselves lost in the woods, a scary place for anyone—let alone two small children—to be at night. What is worse, they then have to face the wicked witch, use skill to outsmart her, escape, and find their way home. To our ancestors this was a tale about facing fear, in particular the dangers lurking in those ancient forests of old. They would have been scared about entering the forest, but they realized that they had to face their fear because they needed to hunt and forage to survive. What better way to inspire confidence than to make up stories where people just like them (or, in the case of Hansel and Gretel, more vulnerable) found themselves in the forest facing hidden dangers. Instead of fearing the unknown, they embraced it and emerged from the undergrowth strong, empowered, and ready to fight another day! Such stories are littered with human tricksters; they might be imbued with magical powers, but they teach us that sometimes fear is a good thing, and that even things that don't go our way at first may work out perfectly in the end.

A trickster and a hero, Jack—in
his original form, as a character from
Appalachian folk tales—is a farm boy who achieves
success through luck, bravado, and often deceitful means.
These tales are part of a strong oral tradition and were recounted
through song and storytelling. Appalachian Jack shares characteristics
with the Jack of English folk tales, but instead of a king, the authority
figure against whom he is pitted is usually a sheriff; Jack is not a prince or the

APPALACHIAN JACK

son of a nobleman, but a poor working boy. Hapless and lazy, Jack relies on his natural
easygoing charm and a dose of good luck to ensure his exploits achieve a successful
outcome . It's true to say that Jack had the "luck of the Devil" in that fortune would
often swing his way. An archetype that represents "everyman," Jack is the joker in us
all. As the famous phrase has it, he's "Jack of all trades, master of none," which hints
at his foolish nature. Like many other famous tricksters, Jack has a way with words.
In one tale, "Lazy Jack and his Calf Skin," Jack convinces his greedy brothers that
he has killed his calf and sold the hide for great riches. His brothers believe him,
and so kill their own animals too, but they fail to sell the skins. In another
tale, Jack, who is living with a woman and her three daughters, receives
help from a bull, which gives him food from its horns. The girls are
sent out to spy on Jack, but he manages to trick them into falling
asleep by playing his fiddle. Such is Jack's magnetism
and magic, he has the ability to win people over
with a smile and a few words, or a
choice tune.

TEACHING

Relax, take each moment as it
comes, and greet each day with
a smile. This will help you
increase your charm or attract
good fortune into your life.

RITUAL

Increase your personal magnetism and attract some good luck with this simple ritual. Take a small can of corn, strain the liquid, and put the kernels in a dish. Sprinkle a couple drops of sunflower oil over the corn and mix with your fingers. As you do this, picture yourself looking and feeling fabulous. Imagine a gold light framing the picture. Take the dish of corn outside and sprinkle the kernels in a wide circle on the ground. Stand in the center of the circle and spin around with your arms outstretched, like a human scarecrow. Say out loud or in your head, "Fortune is mine, from this moment in time. I embrace my fate and I celebrate all that is me and all that is fun. I radiate power and shine like the sun!" Repeat this chant as many times as you like, and, if you feel inspired, skip around the circle as you do so. The key with this ritual is to embrace the playful spirit of Appalachian Jack.

MAGICAL PRACTICE

Attract good fortune into your home by tapping into the element of air and Jack's musical powers. Hang wind chimes in windows around your house; also hang beads, crystals, and anything else that's likely to jangle in the breeze. If you have a tree in your yard, hang a bell on a piece of string from one of the branches.

TRICKSTER TIPS

Introduce corn into your diet. Not only is it nutritious, but it will also help you tap into the magic of Appalachian Jack. As you eat, visualize yourself bathed in the light of the sun.

ASSOCIATIONS

Element EARTH/FIRE
General *Fiddles, pipes, flutes, horns, mountains, bulls, cows, straw, corn*
Stone Slate/granite

The legendary outlaw and
rebellious bandit Robin Hood
epitomizes many aspects of the trickster. He
mocked the rich, robbing them of their treasures in
order to give to the poor. He was a master of disguise, not

ROBIN HOOD

only using Sherwood Forest as
his home and hiding place, but
also having the ability to dress up and pretend to be someone else.
Associated with the Green Man, the protective spirit of the forest, and
also with Herne the Hunter, an antlered spirit and another
manifestation of the Green Man, Robin felt most at home in the woods,
supposedly making the famous Major Oak his home. Robin was a
skilled archer, and he and his merry men were experienced fighters,
also able to wield sword and staff. Confident and sometimes cocky,
this trickster character was thought to have noble blood. He had the
ability to rouse the masses, and inspired confidence in the poor
and the vulnerable. In the Errol Flynn movie *The Adventures of
Robin Hood* (1938), Prince John says, "By my faith, you're a
bold rascal. Robin, I like you." This phrase captures
the essence of what has made this trickster so
well-loved throughout history.

TEACHING

Develop your sense of fun and
rebelliousness to inspire others,
develop leadership skills, and
give your natural allure a boost.

RITUAL

To increase your strength and personal power, try this ritual. Find a quiet spot
outside, somewhere near a tree, preferably an oak. Stand with your back against
the trunk of the tree, your palms pressed against the bark. Take a deep breath in
and imagine the energy of the mighty tree seeping through your skin. Feel your
palms tingling and your back straightening as the tree's energy surges through your
system. It will help you feel confident and self-assured. Look up into the highest
branches and say, "By the power of feisty Robin, my courage holds fast. By the
power of Mother Nature, I lead with passion to the last." Finish by feeling the
strength of the tree supporting you. Enjoy the experience of being close to nature.

Gather up any twigs or acorns that fell to the ground while you performed the ritual. When you get home, create a display using the fruits of the tree, and any other plants or flowers you like. Place a piece of agate in the center of your creation to enhance your connection to the natural world.

MAGICAL PRACTICE

To help you achieve your dreams, draw a large circle in the middle of a piece of paper. Inside the circle, write a short sentence that sums up your heart's desire, such as "To meet my soul mate" or "To be successful in my career." Pin the paper to a bulletin board, and pretend that you're an archer and this is your bull's-eye. Take a deep breath, draw your imaginary arrow, and aim for the heart!

ASSOCIATIONS

Element EARTH

General *Woodland, trees (especially the oak), arrows, feathers, the colors green and brown*

Stone Agate/hematite

This trickster character pops
up in tales from the Cree Native
Americans of Canada. The name of this hero

WHISKEY JACK

and rascal is spelled in numerous ways, and he is also portrayed
differently. Thought to be a friend and supporter of humankind, he
uses his mercurial flair to teach moral lessons. In some tales Whiskey
Jack was created by the Earth, and in others by the Great Spirit; some
stories suggest that he is the son of the mythical Rolling Head
monster, and that he had to kill his mother in order to survive. He is a
joker, with the ability to transform himself and others. In one story
Whiskey Jack shortens the wolverine's legs after it hides Jack's fire
bag and hangs it from a tree. Interestingly, Whiskey Jack was at
first believed to be a troublemaker, creating a
great flood to wipe out the population of
the world, but as folklore progressed
he changed his ways, and ultimately
he plays tricks in order to teach
important truths.

RITUAL

If you'd like to reinvent some part of yourself or your
life, try this ritual. On the night of a full moon, take
a black candle and a white candle. The black represents
the past and the things you'd like to leave behind, for
example anger or fear; the white represents the future
and the things you'd like to invite into your life, for
example love or confidence. Light both candles and say,
"I balance black with white, I reinvent myself this night.
By the power of Whiskey Jack, I look forward not back."
Take a glass containing a splash of whiskey and toast
Whiskey Jack before taking a sip to seal the ritual. (If
you're not a fan of this drink, use apple juice.) Leave
the remaining whiskey out overnight as a mark of
respect for the trickster. As each candle burns down,
consider the new you and see yourself enjoying life!

TEACHING

It's never too late to change, renew, and reinvent yourself.

MAGICAL PRACTICE

Whiskey Jack loves to inhabit woodland and has an affinity with most animals, so if you want to tap into his magic, spend some time outdoors. Feed the birds, take a walk in the park, or volunteer to help out at an animal sanctuary.

TRICKSTER TIPS

Take the ritual a step further by leaving an offering out for Whiskey Jack every night—something small, such as a measure of whiskey, a piece of wood to represent the forests he loves, or a black feather to represent the jay, the bird with which he's associated. Ask Jack to renew your mind and spirit and bless you with his magic.

ASSOCIATIONS

Element FIRE

General *Flint, fire, all creatures (particularly the jay), whiskey, forests, trees*

Stone Apache tears

The Bamapana is a trickster character associated with northern Australia, in particular the Yolngu people of the Northern Territory. He features in Aboriginal

BAMAPANA (bam-a-PAN-a)

tales and is known for his love of bad language. He enjoys pushing the boundaries of acceptable behavior and making people feel uncomfortable. In some tales he's a hero, and in others a despicable character abhorred by his peers. It is thought that he broke many taboos within the clans, and was well-known for his lustful behavior with the ladies. The tribes believed that any squabbles or general discord could be put down to Bamapana's influence! In some tales Bamapana appears to be a hapless fool who is always merry and often reckless, giving him a reputation for craziness. He is a master of contradiction, and so it's hard to pin him down.

RITUAL

Language is the key to Bamapana's magic. He enjoys playing with words and expressing himself in new and exciting ways, which can cause alarm. Light a candle and spend some time thinking about your favorite words. Say them out loud and consider why you like using them and how they make you feel. Now think about a word that sums up what you'd like from life. For example, if you're seeking excitement you might say "adventure" or "action." Write the word down, then, beside it, write another that describes the same thing. Continue writing down words that describe the kind of life you'd like to create. Push the boundaries and go for words you wouldn't normally use. Repeat these words out loud in a positive affirmation, such as, "I create more adventure/action/spontaneity/excitement in my life every day." Pin the paper on a bulletin board or somewhere prominent and, every day, go through the words and repeat the affirmation. Emphasize each word and put some emotion into it.

TEACHING

Be spontaneous, push boundaries, and throw caution to the wind. Step out of your comfort zone to liberate yourself from unhappy situations or increase the fun and adventure in your life.

MAGICAL PRACTICE

Embrace the spirit of Bamapana by doing something you wouldn't usually do every day. Something simple such as smiling at a stranger or taking a different route home from work, can open up a world of magical opportunities!

TRICKSTER TIPS

To keep the energy alive and help to create movement, remember to add new words to your list. You might also want to include images to go with the words and enhance the description. Look out for pictures in magazines that you can use to provide visual stimulation.

ASSOCIATIONS

Element AIR
General *Words, dancing, laughter, shouting*
Stone Quartz/opal

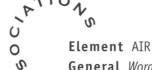

These child-sized people, also
called "the little people," are a popular
myth of the Cree Native Americans. They have
huge eyes and lanky arms and legs. Most commonly
seen lurking near rivers, between the rocks, they're thought

THE MANNEGISHI
(may-may-GWAY-See)

to be aquatic. Folklore suggests that they appear only to children and
medicine people, but there have been many reports of normal people
seeing them, too. Known as pranksters, they are particularly fond of
capsizing canoes and boats. They're associated with water and are
thought to absorb oxygen instead of breathing it. The Mannegishi rarely
speak, but when they do their voices are reported to sound like the
whine of a dragonfly. They're also associated with butterflies.
These magical tricksters prefer to communicate using telepathy,
sending visions and thoughts when you least expect it.
According to storytellers, they spend their time
carving and painting on rocks near rivers and
streams, and they travel in tiny canoes
carved from stone.

RITUAL

If you're looking for insight or hoping to hone your intuition, tap into the element
of water and the magic of the Mannegishi. Take a bowl, preferably a black one, and
fill it with fresh water. Massage a couple drops of lavender essential oil into the
middle of your forehead to stimulate the third eye chakra. Close your eyes and make
a silent wish to the Mannegishi. Ask the little people to bless you with a vision that
will help you in your current situation. Open your eyes and let your gaze fall on the
water. Breathe deeply and let any thoughts or images drift into your mind. If you're
struggling, close your eyes again and imagine you're sitting beside a rock pool. Stir
the water with your left hand and peer into the depths. You may see a symbol,
picture, or pattern developing. When you've finished, stand in the shower and pour
the bowl of water over you. Imagine you're standing beneath a natural fountain,
and enjoy the refreshing sensations as the watery energy pours through the top of
your head. Remember to give thanks to the little people for any insights that
you've received.

TEACHING

Develop your psychic skills, trust your intuition, and listen to your emotions to help you find a way forward.

MAGICAL PRACTICE

Devote part of your yard to the little people. If you don't have one, create a window box and dedicate it to them. Decorate stones with symbols that represent the things you'd like in your life—for example a sun for happiness, a star for success, or a heart for love—and scatter them in this space. Also include white flowers and a piece of aquamarine to represent the element of water.

TRICKSTER TIPS

You can perform the same ritual outside, by a river, pond, or stream. The natural power of free-flowing water will help your psychic skills flourish. Take a crystal or flower with you and drop it into the water as gift to say thanks when you've finished.

ASSOCIATIONS

Element WATER

General *Rivers, streams, dragonflies, butterflies, rocks, dreams*

Stone Aquamarine

According to legend, it was in
the year 1284 that a mysterious man appeared
in the German town of Hamelin, claiming that he
could cure the infestation of rats in return for a sum of money.
The townsfolk agreed, and the character, dressed in a bright coat of
many colors, produced a pipe and began to play. The rats gathered

THE PIED PIPER

around him, and he led them on a dance out of the town and into the river, where they
drowned. The townsfolk, however, went back on their word and did not pay the strange
man. The Pied Piper, as we know him from folklore, was angry, and returned to the town
later that year dressed as a huntsman wearing a red hat. This time, when he played his
pipe the children of the town followed him, and were never seen again. The story is famous
as a nursery rhyme and fable, but its origins are sketchy. It is said that 130 children
disappeared that day, in an event that became known as the "children's exodus." Some
might say the outcome of the story was fair, considering the townsfolk had deceived the
piper by not honoring their agreement. It is thought the children were led into a hole in
the middle of a hill, suggesting that the Pied Piper was part fey and able to transport
the children into the fairy otherworld. The mystical piper was never seen again,
making him the ultimate trickster. Confident, mercurial, and with magical
powers, he transfixed humans and animals alike with his beautiful playing. A
performer who initially enjoyed the limelight, he adorned his brightly
colored coat to demonstrate his extraordinary gift. He was able to
adapt his talents to good and evil, depending on his mood.
Although supposedly human, he could transform his
attire and shift between worlds, like some of
the more powerful trickster gods.

TEACHING

Have the courage to seek
justice and the confidence
to speak your truth, whether
you need to solve a sticky
problem or just want to boost
your allure.

This simple ritual will help to focus your mind, organize your thoughts, and help you speak the truth. Put on some music that you like, something with a steady, rhythmic beat. Clear a space and begin to tap your feet alternately while considering the problem at hand. Once you've got a rhythm, begin to march to the beat, first on the spot and then around the room. As you do so, imagine you're drawing a figure eight with your feet. Each time you go over the figure, it gets brighter and bigger and reinforces your personal power. It will soon become second nature to follow the pattern without thinking about it, leaving your mind free to organize and ponder. Repeat the pattern until the song finishes. Finally, grab a notebook and write down any thoughts or ideas that have come to mind during or after the ritual. The physical activity of plotting a pattern will steady and settle your mind, allowing your subconscious to work creatively on the problem.

MAGICAL PRACTICE

If you want to feel more confident, take inspiration from the Pied Piper. Change your clothes to suit the occasion. As a showman he wore a brightly colored coat, so take a look at your wardrobe and introduce some brighter shades. Warm colors like red, gold, and orange increase self-esteem, even if you only include a splash here and there.

TRICKSTER TIPS

It's not always easy to carry out this ritual if you're in public without getting some strange stares! So, if you need a quick fix, simply imagine doing it in your mind. See yourself tracing out the pattern as you march to the beat. Alternatively, trace the figure eight on its side on a piece of paper and go over the pattern with your finger while counting out a beat in your head.

ASSOCIATIONS

Element EARTH/AIR

General *Pipe, music, red hat, bright colors, fairy mounds and hills*

Stone Carnelian/garnet/ red jasper

The Saci is a Brazilian prankster in the form of a one-legged dwarf, who causes havoc around the home. He has holes in the palms of both hands and smokes a pipe. He also wears a magical red cap or hat,

THE SACI (sa-SI)

which helps him to disappear and reappear whenever he chooses. It's thought that if you can steal the Saci's cap, he will grant you a wish. Known for hiding things around the house and tormenting pets, the Saci tends to play tricks that are harmless but annoying. His favorite treat is tobacco for his pipe, and those who feel under threat from a Saci may leave a supply out at night to appease him. The Saci is a master juggler and is known for juggling hot coals, which fall through the holes in his hands. He's also thought to be able to transform into a matim-taperê, a bird with a haunting cry. Lively and agile, the Saci is almost impossible to catch, despite having only one leg; he doesn't like crossing flowing water, however. Folklore has it that if you see a swirl of dust, it is probably an invisible Saci running through your home.

TEACHING

Be flexible in body and mind, so that you can juggle the many different roles you have to fulfill every day. Boost your energy to help you cope with a mountain of tasks.

RITUAL

To create a harmonious, easygoing atmosphere at home, try this simple ritual. Take a small paintbrush and a dish, and spend a few minutes brushing brick dust from the walls of your home into the dish. When you've gathered a small pile, add a pinch of paprika and mix with your fingers. Visualize your home as a happy place, with everyone getting on and enjoying life together. Take the magical powder and sprinkle it around the boundaries of your home. If you live in an apartment, sprinkle a little of the powder beneath your welcome mat and on window ledges. As you do this, say, "I eliminate all stress, may the days fly past with ease. I welcome joy and light, as the Saci I appease." Repeat this ritual once a month to ensure the flow of positive energy into your home.

TRICKSTER TIPS

Dust a little of your ritual powder on the soles of your shoes for protection and to help you move smoothly through the day. Remember to repeat the magical chant as you do so, and to visualize the day going well. This is particularly effective if you're facing an obstacle or a challenge.

MAGICAL PRACTICE

The Saci credits his red cap with giving him the power to move quickly from one place to another. Invest in a hat that you like, and leave a quartz crystal inside it overnight. In the morning, don the hat and imagine a small red ball of light hovering over the center of your scalp, giving you energy, clarity, and the ability to think on your feet!

ASSOCIATIONS

Element EARTH
General *Pipe, tobacco, dust, red hat or cap, coal, red beads*
Stone Quartz/any red stone

This mercurial character
features in stories from the Middle Ages.
Originating in Middle Low German, his tales were
transmitted both orally and then in written form
throughout Germany and Denmark. This prankster and

TILL EULENSPIEGEL
(till ol-lun-shpee-gul)

comedian is often pictured carrying an owl and a mirror, and for that reason was
commonly called "owlglass." It is claimed that the bones of the real Till
Eulenspiegel lay in a coffin adorned with an owl and a mirror, in the town of
Lauenberg. Associated with craftsmen, who bore the weight of his banter, Till did
not differentiate between the working class and the nobility, playing jokes on
both sides whenever it took his fancy. A master of communication, he was
known for his ability to play with language and cause arguments through its
misuse. One of his common nicknames is "wipe the ass," a nod to the
bawdy nature of some of his tales, which frequently had to be rewritten
to appeal to children. In one story, the child Till rides behind his
father, exposing his bare behind to all they pass on the journey.
In another, an older version of Till tricks a priest into
soiling the palm of his hand with feces. Dressed as
a jester, Till pokes fun at anyone who takes
themselves too seriously.

RITUAL

Invite the spirit of joy into your life with this simple ritual inspired by Till. Take a
hand mirror and place it outside in the light of the midday sun. Leave it there for
five minutes. When you retrieve it, wrap it in an orange or red scarf. Take an
orange candle, and with a knife carve an image of the sun into the wax. Light the
candle and spend a few minutes breathing deeply. Clear your mind of any clutter.
Remove the mirror from the scarf and hold it in both hands. Gaze into the glass
and imagine that, instead of your reflection, you see the sun floating on the
surface. Close your eyes and visualize the sun's rays passing through the glass and
bathing you in golden light. Say, "Light of the world, bless me upon this day,
illuminate my path and show me the way. Brighten my thoughts, words, and
deeds. For future happiness, I sow the seeds!" Wrap the mirror in the scarf once
more and let the candle burn down while you picture yourself sitting in the warm
glow of a beautiful sunset.

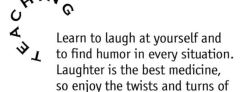

TEACHING

Learn to laugh at yourself and to find humor in every situation. Laughter is the best medicine, so enjoy the twists and turns of life and make time to have fun.

MAGICAL PRACTICE

As a reminder to laugh in the face of adversity and seek the humor in every situation, carry the Joker from a pack of playing cards in your pocket. Look at it every morning and say, "Come what may, I will laugh today!"

TRICKSTER TIPS

If you want to tap into your innate wisdom and embrace your intuition, carve an owl shape into the wax of the candle before carrying out the ritual, and substitute the word "happiness" with "wisdom." Imagine that when you look into the mirror, you're looking through the enormous eyes of an owl.

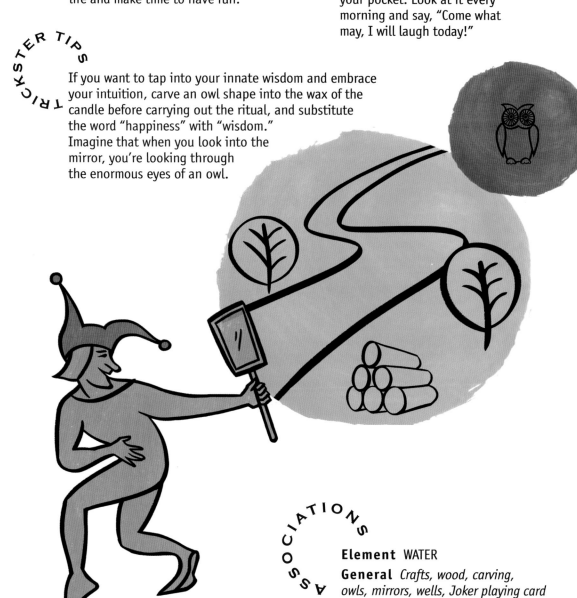

ASSOCIATIONS

Element WATER
General *Crafts, wood, carving, owls, mirrors, wells, Joker playing card*
Stone Fool's gold (iron pyrite)

This trickster character features in tales told by the Winnebago tribe of Nebraska. This rebellious chief went against all the rules. His name means "tricky one," and he has a devil-may-care attitude to match. One story tells how Wakdjunkaga is determined to go to war, but, being chief, is forbidden

WAKDJUNKAGA (wack-junk-ka-ga)

to go himself. Nothing will deter him, and so, instead of attending the special feast that has been prepared in advance of the battle, Wakdjunkaga decides to spend his time with a woman, which is against tribal rules. When finally the hour comes to fight, he does everything possible to dissuade his warriors from going with him, including stamping on weapons and talismans. In the end they are so appalled by his behavior that they leave him to it. Wakdjunkaga is known for his voracious appetite. Lusty and a lover of women, he also enjoys his food, and spends most of his time tricking various animals into his cooking pot. In one tale, he entices a group of ducks to join him in a dancing game. He encourages them to keep their eyes tightly shut, and one by one he wrings their necks. He often appears silly, as in one ludicrous tale that involves his right arm fighting his left for food! Despite this, Wakdjunkaga did learn from his mistakes. He went on to curb his appetites, even claiming a wife and having many children. He was known for his humility, accepting that at times he could be foolish. He spent his remaining days protecting the Earth and his people from evil spirits.

RITUAL

Protect yourself and those you love with this simple ritual. In a pot or cauldron over a medium heat, steep a handful of fresh sage and rosemary leaves in hot water with some chopped onion and a pinch of salt and pepper. When the water is simmering and giving off sage-scented steam, take a large feather and waft the vapor around your body. As you do so, imagine a protective black shell forming around you. The shell rebuffs any negative energy, sending it back wherever it came from. Carry the pot through your home, wafting the vapor as you go, and imagining your entire home and everyone in it surrounded by a giant black shell. Again, the shell acts as a shield against harmful energy. Strain the liquid and use it as a stock for a tasty vegetable soup. Sip the soup while picturing the shell around your home and loved ones. Rinse out the cooking pot and, whenever you use it, visualize the protective shell.

TEACHING

Accept your faults and adopt a spirit of forgiveness, to release guilt and protect yourself and others.

MAGICAL PRACTICE

Lapis lazuli can help you find your true path. Hold a piece in your left hand as you ask Wakdjunkaga for inspiration. Place it under your pillow for prophetic dreams.

TRICKSTER TIPS

There's something magical about preparing food, and Wakdjunkaga loved eating. Every time you cook, imagine you're infusing the food with love and healing energy to get the most out of the meal. Picture each plate surrounded by gold light, and think about the goodness of each ingredient of the meal.

ASSOCIATIONS

Element EARTH

General *Sage, rosemary, hawks, food in general, cooking pots*

Stone Lapis lazuli

Taking It Further

Human tricksters are an interesting breed. They have the same characteristics as their supernatural counterparts, and in some cases they do have magical powers, but they're more familiar to us in shape and form. This makes it easier for us to identify with them. If you want to delve further into this world, try these top tips.

Engage your imagination. If you were a trickster and you had a magical power, what would it be? Perhaps you'd like to be invisible or to have the ability to run super-fast. Think about why you'd choose that power—what advantage would it give you in your life right now? This is key to uncovering your motivation, and in helping you identify areas of your life that you might want to improve. For example, if you'd like to be able to disappear by clicking your fingers, it could be because you want to shy away from some part of your life, or from yourself. Perhaps you're really searching for a way to escape the drudgery of life or a relationship or situation that you've outgrown? Be honest, and think of practical ways of resolving this. Remember to put your trickster hat on and ask, "What would the trickster do in this situation?"

Have a laugh. Most of the human trickster characters enjoy a good giggle. They poke fun at themselves and others. When was the last time you laughed out loud? If it's been a while, do something about it. Invest in a box set of your favorite comedy, or get together with friends and have some fun. Embracing playfulness is a powerful part of trickster magic!

Take up a new skill. Tricksters are mercurial characters, and they have a number of talents that they use to their advantage. If you want to tap into this potent energy, you need to look at your strengths and broaden your existing skills. Go for fun things that you've always wanted to try but never got around to, such as learning how to juggle or dance the tango. Remember that the trickster archetype encourages us to be spontaneous and to seek pleasure in all things.

56

CHAPTER THREE

Deity

Tricksters

Tricksters come in many shapes and forms, but none is more powerful than a trickster deity. These gods and goddesses have the power of creation on their side. Often ruling the elements and the planets, and causing chaos in the heavens, these characters have potent powers of persuasion, which they use on us and one another. They represent fate, and the fact that there are some things we just can't change when destiny steps in and turns everything on its head. Our ancestors used these deities as a way to explain sudden changes in fortune, believing their influence played a part in creating both magic and mayhem, and that these deities were instrumental in shaping the future. They would petition the gods in the hope that they could bring about positive change and improve situations.

Commonly seen as messengers, trickster gods have the ability to travel between realms, dabbling in the real world and in the world of illusion. Sometimes they travel between this world and the next, governing the elements of life and death. They don't confine their mischief-making to Earth; they also like to play with the gods, causing conflict, confusion, and sometimes success. There's always an element of chance to their actions. Fun and flighty, these mercurial characters feature in the most entertaining tales. They show us that a lighthearted approach to life is essential, and that if we think outside the norm, we will always find options and solutions. Keep an open mind when working with trickster deities. Invite their energy into your life when you need a youthful burst of energy, or a frivolous attitude.

One of the most powerful trickster gods, the Norse god Loki is the son of the frost giant. Mischievous and malicious at times, Loki brings trouble but also

L O K I (Low-ki)

solutions. Many of the other deities called on him when they needed help, because he was resourceful and known for his ingenuity. But more often than not, his solutions provided more problems. It's thought that Loki caused the end of the world of the gods by being responsible for the death of Baldr. Frigg, Baldr's mother and the wife of the god Odin, went to great lengths to bring him back by asking everyone to weep for his soul, but Loki refused to show pity, resigning the god to the realm of the dead forever. Baldr was seen to represent everything light and good in the world, and his death brought about the start of Ragnarok, a long, dark winter and the end of all things. Contrary and extrovert, Loki enjoys being different. He celebrates his uniqueness and goes on to mate with the giantess Angrboda, creating three hideous monster children—Hel, the goddess of the grave; Jormungand, the great serpent; and Fenrir, the wolf who kills Odin during Ragnarok. A skilled shape-shifter, Loki can change into any form and often does so as a way of fooling people.

TEACHING

Transform your life by recognizing your unique gifts and learning to love yourself just as you are. Celebrate your successes and be true to yourself at all times.

RITUAL

Unleash your potential with this ritual. The image of entwined snakes is often associated with Loki, and snakes have transformative powers that can enhance his magic. Take a red candle for action, and with a pin carve the image of a snake into the wax. Loop a string of red beads or a length of red cotton loosely around the base of the candle, to represent the serpent Jormungand. Light the candle and, as it burns down, imagine you're like a snake shedding your skin. See yourself stepping out of the shadows and emerging into bright light. Say, "I am transformed, in the light. I love myself, my future's bright!" Spend a few minutes in quiet contemplation and let any thoughts or ideas come into your mind. They may be pointing you in a new direction, so make a note of anything significant.

MAGICAL PRACTICE

When you need a confidence boost, picture someone you admire and imagine you're that person. How would they deal with the situation in which you find yourself? Would they approach it with optimism and strength? Try to imagine walking in their shoes. Finally, place your hands on your heart and imagine tapping into your inner confidence. See yourself glowing with the power and ability to achieve anything!

TRICKSTER TIPS

Keep the beads or string that you used in the ritual with you, worn on your wrist or around your neck as a charm to help you feel confident and to remind you that you can transform yourself at any point. Carrying a piece of carnelian will also help you tap into Loki's power, and enhance your personal magnetism.

ASSOCIATIONS

Element WATER
General *Wolves, horses, serpents, snow and frost, the planet Jupiter*
Stone Carnelian/red jasper

HERMES

Hermes is best known for his role as the Greek messenger god (the Roman Mercury). Fleet of foot, he is the bringer of good fortune, but also a master thief who would steal precious items from the other deities and hide them for fun. He's often called the god of thieves. This mercurial trickster brought the dead to the underworld, and governed commerce and music; the phrase "Jack of all trades" fits him, and it's true to say that the other deities couldn't pin him down. He is often pictured carrying a staff, winged and wearing a cloak and sandals to speed his passage. Clever and resourceful, Hermes demonstrated his ingenuity when, as a child, he stole cattle from the god Apollo, hiding their tracks by tying bark to their hoofs. A deceitful, secretive deity, Hermes is nevertheless generally thought to be helpful, particularly to humankind, bringing messages from the dead and traveling between worlds.

RITUAL

Turn up the charm and increase your personal magnetism using the power of Hermes. First, you'll need to find a stick that you can use in the same way that Hermes uses his caduceus. This could be a walking stick or cane, or a branch that has fallen from a tree. Start by standing with your feet hip-width apart. Hold the stick in both hands and breathe deeply until you feel relaxed. Imagine that with every out-breath, a pair of huge white wings begin to unfurl from your shoulder blades. Feel the wings extend outward, spreading until they fill the entire space. Raise the stick until it is pointing out in front of you. Imagine that it's a powerful staff, sending rays of golden light out into the world. If you have a particular aim in mind, for example if there is someone you want to impress, imagine directing a ray of light from the staff toward them. Say, "I shine my light with confidence."

TEACHING

Think on your feet and learn how to turn on the charm in any situation. Communicate well to deliver an effective message and attract admiration.

MAGICAL PRACTICE

For inspiration and to unleash your creativity, tap into the power of Hermes by playing your favorite dance track and getting lost in the music! Imagine the tune is taking you on a journey, and that you are soaring through the heavens.

TRICKSTER TIPS

You can also use your ritual staff to create a protective circle, if you're feeling under pressure or need a boost. Just imagine drawing a circle of light around you with the staff. Picture a shower of golden light, like a spotlight bathing you in energy and filling the circle.

ASSOCIATIONS

Element AIR
General *Wings, the caduceus (winged staff), music, pipes, tortoises*
Stone Fool's gold (iron pyrite)

PAN

This Greek trickster god and lord of the wood and huntsmen governs music, dance, laughter, and merriment. He's also linked to sexual desire, and was thought to be a strong opponent of marriage. His name, which means "all-encompassing," also provides the origin of the word "panic," which means "out of mind." Pan believed there was nothing wrong with stepping outside of your comfort zone, throwing caution to the wind, embracing chaos, and letting go of fear. Often called "lord of the beasts," he governs and protects the natural world and everything in it. He's associated with wild animals, and is often pictured as half-man, half-goat. Known for his love of music and of women, Pan could play the flute and the panpipes. The latter were created when he made advances toward a nymph called Syrinx. She rebuffed him and turned herself into reeds, which became Pan's pipes and the instrument we know today. Interestingly, the Christian Church chose to demonize the image of Pan, giving him horns and suggesting that he was associated with the Devil, probably because of his raucous reputation!

RITUAL

Face your fears with this simple ritual. Add a couple drops of rosemary essential oil to a bowl of hot water. Place a towel over your head, close your eyes, and inhale the vapor from the hot water. Breathe in and out deeply until you feel relaxed and focused. Picture a forest in your mind. See the wild undergrowth and the tall trees, and imagine you're standing in the deepest part of this woodland. You see a chink of sunlight filtering through the branches and bathing you in warmth and vitality. Now that you're feeling energized and powerful, think about the one thing you're afraid of; this could be a person or a situation. Imagine there's a framed picture of this fear leaning against a tree in front of you. As you step closer, the picture reduces in size, until eventually it's a tiny pinprick of light. Now picture it flying away into the sky. Thank Pan for helping you face your fear, and slowly imagine the forest slipping away, until you're focused on your breathing again. Remove the towel and sprinkle the water outside.

TRICKSTER TIPS

If possible, try the ritual visualization in a real forest or patch of woodland, or even your yard. Instead of using a bowl of scented water, take a sprig of fresh rosemary and inhale its natural aroma. Getting close to nature will help you tap into Pan's magical energy and feel nurtured and secure.

MAGICAL PRACTICE

Blow away the cobwebs and feel invigorated by tapping into Pan's element. On a windy day, open all the windows in your home and let the breeze blow through and clear the air. Stand outside with your arms outstretched and spin around. Say, "I am cleansed and rejuvenated by the power of Pan!"

TEACHING

Let go of preconceived ideas, take a chance, and abandon easy familiarity. Face your fears, and, most importantly, have fun and seize the day.

ASSOCIATIONS

Element AIR
General *Wind instruments, panpipes, reeds, woods and forests, horns, wild animals*
Stone Ruby/agate

Lugh, often called Lugus, is the Celtic trickster god of light and the harvest. A slippery character, Lugh was also called "the shining one." He governs trade and industry, and is a master at crafts, good with his hands and nimble on his feet. Similar to the Roman god Mercury and

L U G H (loo)

his Greek counterpart Hermes, Lugh was a skilled craftsman and able to wield a weapon in battle. One famous tale tells how Lugh, who was charming and somewhat arrogant, arrives at the hall of the high kings of Ireland. The guard explains that only one person with a particular talent can be granted admission: one blacksmith, one warrior, and so on. Lugh runs through the list of all his talents, but the guard replies each time that they already have someone with each skill. Lugh beams confidently and says, "You may have one person who can do each of those things, but do you have one person who can do all of them?" Another Jack of all trades, Lugh is eventually allowed to enter the castle. He always carried with him a magical spear, which could shoot fire and attack by itself.

TEACHING

Be confident and celebrate your unique talents. Nurture your special gifts and shine your light whenever possible.

MAGICAL PRACTICE

Bread is associated with Lugh because of its connection to wheat and the harvest. Take a slice of bread and sprinkle the crumbs outdoors for the birds. Say, "I nurture the land and it nurtures me!"

Invite Lugh's power into your life, and embrace your creative talents by making an altar in your home. Find a table or shelf, preferably somewhere light and airy, and dress it with orange and white candles to represent the sun, a bowl of fresh fruit or vegetables to represent the harvest, and a knife or dagger to represent Lugh's magical spear. Place images of the sun in this space, and a piece of citrine and/or topaz. Stags are also associated with this trickster deity, so include ornaments and images of stags. Take a wooden box and place it in the center of the altar. Light the candles and spend a few minutes thinking about your own gifts and talents. What are you good at? What do you enjoy doing? How would you like to see these gifts develop? In other words, how will you harvest your talents? Take a piece of paper and write down a positive statement about the future, for example: "I am an accomplished musician. I write songs that people love to hear, and I am successful." Place the wish in the wooden box with the citrine and/or topaz. Every week, add a new positive statement to the box, and remember to keep updating the altar by adding new things. This will encourage the magical energy to flow freely, promoting movement and action in your life.

TRICKSTER TIPS

As you start to embrace your hidden talents, you'll notice small successes and achievements. Make a note of them, and add them to your wooden wish box. Make a point of thanking Lugh for this sudden burst of creativity and for increasing your confidence.

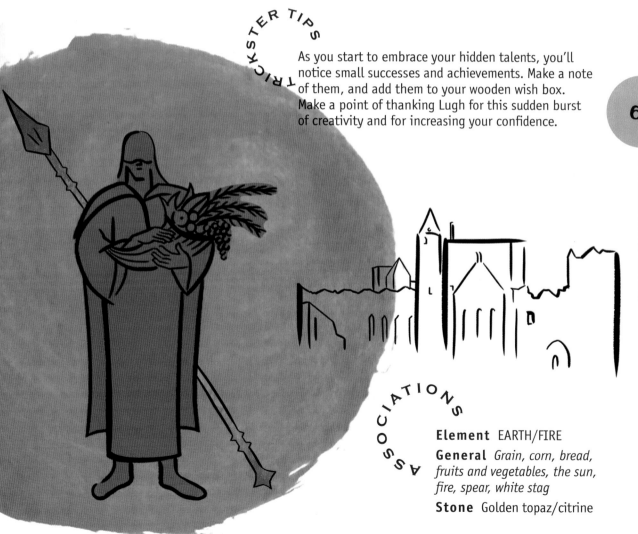

ASSOCIATIONS

Element EARTH/FIRE

General *Grain, corn, bread, fruits and vegetables, the sun, fire, spear, white stag*

Stone *Golden topaz/citrine*

This Greek goddess of chaos knew how to throw the cat among the pigeons. She delighted in inciting trouble and conflict, and took great amusement from the strife she caused. Her Roman name, Discordia, means "discord," and although her character sounds far from pleasant, she was an essential member of the Greek pantheon. Eris knew that the other gods took themselves far too seriously, so she found it enjoyable to play with their egos and bring them down a peg or two. As a result she was the only deity not invited to the wedding of Peleus and Thetis. Eris didn't let this stop her however. She turned up anyway, and threw a golden apple into the crowd, inscribed with the words "to the fairest." Three of the goddesses laid claim to the apple, causing confrontation and ultimately sparking the Trojan War. Often pictured carrying a burning torch and with writhing snakes in her hair, Eris was thought to cause quarrels within families. Despite her reputation, she can be viewed in a positive light. Not only did she make the gods question their pride and learn to take themselves less seriously, but also she helped her people express themselves and voice their opinions.

ERIS (EH-ris)

RITUAL

Find your self-belief and face up to change with this tasty ritual. Start by lighting a candle and asking Eris to bless you with her confident, assertive approach to life. Take an apple, a fruit associated with this goddess, core it, and put the seeds to one side. Cut the remaining fruit into quarters, one for each of the directions, north, south, east, and west. Drizzle with honey and place on a baking pan in a medium oven for 10–15 minutes, or until the quarters have turned golden. Before you eat each piece, say, "I love myself and I love my life. I embrace the four directions of my fate." Sprinkle the seeds outdoors in all four directions, repeating the magical affirmation. As you do so, imagine that you are sowing the seeds of your future success.

TRICKSTER TIPS

If you're feeling green-thumbed, take this ritual a step further and, instead of sprinkling the seeds, plant them in a pot. Every day as you water them, repeat the affirmation from the ritual and picture yourself happy and confident!

MAGICAL PRACTICE

For a quick power boost when you're feeling vulnerable, strike a match and hold the flame aloft. Think of Eris holding her torch, shedding light on the world, and speaking her mind. Say, "I ignite my power. I speak my truth."

TEACHING

Be objective and speak your truth when it is appropriate. Finding your own voice and asserting yourself will help you take the twists and turns of fate in your stride.

ASSOCIATIONS

Element FIRE
General *Snakes, torches, the night, daggers, apples, dreams*
Stone Amber

Also known as Elegba or
Legba, Eshu is a trickster god of the
African Yoruba people. He acts as a messenger
between Earth and the sky, carrying messages and
petitions for help to the other gods. Despite this, he is far
from helpful himself, preferring to cause chaos and confusion. He
finds it amusing when the wires get crossed in communication. Sly

E S H U (EH-shu)

and cunning, Eshu enjoys playing
tricks. He was given his messenger
status after stealing some yams from the High God's garden. He made
footprints using the deity's slippers, and claimed that he had stolen them in
order to keep them for himself. This was not well-received, and the High God
ordered that Eshu visit the Earth every day and then return to the sky, in order to
report on daily events. Eshu is a spiritual gatekeeper, and is often called the god
of the crossroads. He is gifted with an eloquent tongue and so brings divine
inspiration. He makes both humankind and deities think by providing them
with just enough information to make them want to find out more. In one
tale, he walks down a path wearing a hat that is red on one side and
black on the other. The villagers on each side of the path see only one
color. After he's gone, an argument starts up between them about
what color the stranger's hat was. Eshu returns and explains
that each half was a different color, teaching the
villagers that perceptions can vary and that we
shouldn't always believe what we see
on the surface.

RITUAL

Perform this ritual when you need spiritual help, or to shed light on a situation.
Take two candles, one red and one black, and stand them side by side. Sprinkle
sugar in a circle around the candles as an offering to Eshu, and light them. The two
colors represent different viewpoints and paths, depending on your question. For
example, red is the color of action, so this candle represents a positive answer and
the black candle represents a negative answer. Ask your question out loud. You
might say, "Should I change my career path?" or "Should I leave this relationship?"
Watch the flames of both candles. If the red flame grows larger than the black, it's
a positive response, and vice versa if the black flame gets bigger. If you don't have
a specific question in mind, gaze at both flames for a few minutes and then close
your eyes. Let any thoughts, words, or images come to you, and make a note of
them; they could be insights that will help you in the future. Let both candles burn
down, and remember to give thanks to Eshu for blessing you with his magic and
helping you see both sides of the story.

TRICKSTER TIPS

Create your own mobile divination kit dedicated to Eshu. Keep two buttons, one red and one black, in a velvet pouch for on-the-spot guidance. Ask your question and then draw a button from the bag—if it's red it's a yes, if it's black it's a no.

MAGICAL PRACTICE

For spiritual insights and visions to help you make decisions, visit a crossroads and—if possible—stand in the center. Leave an offering to Eshu, such as a piece of candy, and ask him you to bless you with the power of perception.

TEACHING

Fire your imagination by asking "What if?" Be open to new ideas and explore all the options.

ASSOCIATIONS

Element AIR/EARTH
General *Crossroads, staffs, pipes, candy, the colors red and black*
Stone Quartz

This Chinese trickster god
always appears as a boy or a youth,
never a fully grown man. This suits his

NEZHA (NEH-za)

reckless, playful
nature. His mother
carried him in her womb for three years, and finally gave
birth to a meatball, which, when cut in two, revealed the boy
fully grown. This stunt sets the precedent for his trickster ways
and gives a flavor of things to come. Nezha has the power to fly
through the sky, and is often pictured with two wheels of fire beneath
his feet and carrying a spear. He also holds a golden hoop known as
the cosmic ring. Originally, Nezha was sent down to Earth to battle a
plague of demons, and because of this he's also seen as a protective
influence. His exploits include setting the sea on fire and killing
the Dragon King's son. But, seeing the error of his ways, Nezha
commits suicide to pay for his sins. In some tales he's
resurrected by a priest who uses lotus blossoms to create
his body, and in others he turns up as a ball of flesh,
which, when sliced apart, reveals his
newly reborn form.

TEACHING

It's never too late to start
again. Don't be afraid of new
beginnings, whether you're
looking for a completely fresh
start or simply want to revamp
your image.

ASSOCIATIONS

Element AIR/FIRE
General *Fire, dragons, lotus flowers,
the ocean, circles, wheels*
Stone Jade

RITUAL

Let go of the past and clear the path for a new beginning by tapping into Nezha's magic. Take a white flower to represent the lotus that healed this deity, and find a stream, river, or pond. If you can't find free-flowing water easily, fill the bathtub with water. Pull the petals off the flower one by one and throw them into the water. Each petal represents a part of your past that you'd like to release, for example a bad habit, a thought, or a memory. As you cast each petal into the water, say, "By the power of Nezha I cast this away. I am reborn another day. A fantastic future I create, by sweeping clean my spiritual slate." Imagine that, as you throw the petal into the water, you're dropping the thought or memory into the sea. Finally, imagine a cleansing ring of fire encircling your body, giving you the strength and energy you need to move forward.

MAGICAL PRACTICE

Carry the Wheel of Fortune tarot card in your pocket as a charm to help you tap into Nezha's magic and to attract good fortune. Visualize yourself sitting on a Ferris wheel, and see it moving upward until you're riding high in the sky!

TRICKSTER TIPS

If you're feeling creative, draw a large white flower and write a word or phrase in each of the petals to represent the things you wish to let go of. Cut out the flower and burn it, either in a fire or in the flame of a candle, repeating the magical chant of the ritual. This is an effective way to cut emotional ties and give your spirit the freedom to soar!

Known as the god of one
thousand tricks, this powerful, half-
mortal trickster was covered in tattoos. A creator
god who also had the ability to destroy with the flick
of his hand, Maui chose to change things he didn't like or

MAUI (MOU-ee)

understand. In one tale, he lassoes the
sun and fights off the sun god with his
grandmother's magic jawbone, until the sun agrees to move more
slowly through the sky. This gives the people more time to cook, hunt,
and bathe in the sun's rays. Maui also thinks that the sky hangs too low,
and with his immense strength pushes it upward. He is associated with
the ocean and all its bounty. In one tale he goes fishing with his brother,
using his own blood as bait and managing to haul in huge catches, which
become the Polynesian islands. Maui enjoyed playing pranks, but he
also liked to help, and many of his biggest tricks were of benefit to the
human race. Being half-human, Maui was not immortal, so he
hatched a plan to gain immortality. He climbed into the body of
the goddess of death, Hina, in an attempt to pass through it
and be blessed with her gifts, but the goddess was
woken by the sound of a bird and promptly
crushed Maui to death.

RITUAL

Give yourself a boost with this simple but effective ritual. Invite the power of Maui
into your life each day. Throw back the drapes and greet the sun. Stand with your
feet hip-width apart and your palms together over your chest. Take a deep breath in
and push your hands straight up into the air. Let your breath out and bring your
hands apart until your arms are outstretched like a scarecrow. Lower your arms to
your sides and repeat the process. As you breathe in, imagine you're breathing in
the light of the morning sun. As you breathe out, imagine you're expelling any
negative energy. See it as dark smoke filtering from your lungs. Spend a few
minutes every morning performing this ritual. When you've finished, ask Maui to
bless you with strength and ingenuity for the rest of the day!

MAGICAL PRACTICE

This ritual works even if there's little sun in the sky. The key is to visualize yourself bathed in the sun's rays. Feel your skin absorbing the warmth, and imagine a small fire in your chest, providing you with strength and confidence.

Stuck for an answer to a question or a solution to a tricky problem? Go fishing—in your mind, at least. Imagine you're sitting beside a river. Focus on the situation and ask Maui to give you insight. Cast your line into the water, and wait. Let any thoughts or images come to you; you may see them forming on the water's surface, or you may simply pull the idea, like a fish, from the watery depths.

TEACHING

Take time to nurture yourself and lift your spirits to gain strength and comfort and find solutions to your problems.

ASSOCIATIONS

Element WATER/AIR
General *Oceans, fish, the sun, tattoos*
Stone Ocean jasper

This Aztec god of chaos,
discord, and change is the ultimate
trickster, tempting others with his powers and
causing conflict and disruption. In particular, he liked

TEZCATLIPOCA (tes-KAHT-li-poh-kah)

to change shape, causing confusion among mortals and deities
alike. In one tale he disguises himself and encourages one of the
other gods to get drunk and seduce his own sister. The Aztecs thought
he was the first god and creator of the earth, a primal force, and that all
the other deities were therefore aspects of his power. Tezcatlipoca
governs the night and is sometimes called Lord of the North. He's
also thought to be associated with sorcery. Often depicted in the
form of a jaguar, he fights the god Quetzalcoatl in one tale, and
transforms into this creature. His name means
"smoking mirror," perhaps from the black obsidian
the Aztec priests used to predict the future.
Tezcatlipoca is a busy god, and governs
many areas, including the sky and the
Earth, warriors, and magic.

RITUAL

This ritual will help you tap into Tezcatlipoca's magic and make the most of daily
opportunities. Wrap a hand mirror in a piece of black satin, and leave it on a window
ledge overnight. In the morning, remove the mirror from the satin and hold it in
both hands. Gaze at your reflection and smile. Notice how this one expression lights
up your face. Say into the mirror, "With confidence and flair, I enter this day.
I shine my power, come what may!" Say this magical phrase as though you mean
it, and repeat it ten times in total, being sure to continue looking at your
reflection. When you've finished, wrap the mirror in the satin and leave it
somewhere prominent. Repeat the affirmation at any point in the day when you feel
under stress or in need of a confidence boost. Also repeat it whenever you catch
sight of your reflection.

TRICKSTER TIPS

If you use a small hand mirror or compact, you can pop it into your purse and bring it out at any point during the day to repeat the ritual. Even if you're in company, you can repeat the magical affirmation in your head rather than saying it out loud, and just pretend you're checking your makeup!

MAGICAL PRACTICE

Tezcatlipoca lost his right foot fighting a monster on Earth, and it was replaced with a black obsidian mirror. Hold a piece of obsidian in your right hand while asking him for guidance and strength. Tezcatlipoca can also help you keep your feet on the ground at all times, and carrying a piece of obsidian will assist you with this.

TEACHING

Embrace the twists and turns of fate, find the courage to stand your ground, and create magical change in your life.

ASSOCIATIONS

Element AIR/EARTH
General *Night, snakes, jaguars, mirrors, the number 10, the colors black and yellow, north*
Stone Obsidian

Taking It Further

If you feel an affinity with trickster deities and enjoy working with their myths and legends, take things further by making their presence felt in every area of your life. Try these top tips and suggestions!

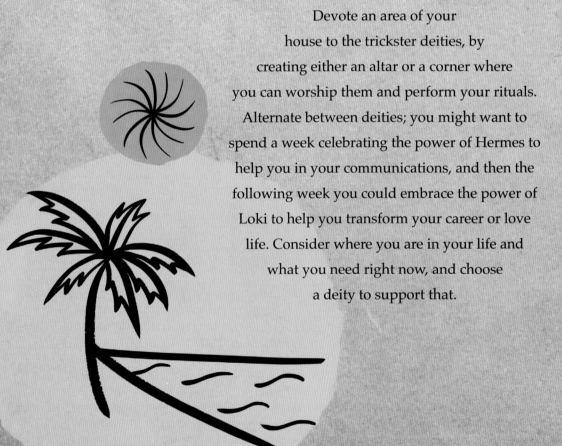

Devote an area of your house to the trickster deities, by creating either an altar or a corner where you can worship them and perform your rituals. Alternate between deities; you might want to spend a week celebrating the power of Hermes to help you in your communications, and then the following week you could embrace the power of Loki to help you transform your career or love life. Consider where you are in your life and what you need right now, and choose a deity to support that.

If you identify with a particular deity, delve into their story and find out more about other characters and tales from that mythology. For example, you might find yourself drawn to Nezha, the Chinese trickster god, so look into other myths and legends to help you tap into his power—by exploring dragon tales, for example, and enhancing your rituals by using the power of the dragon for success and protection.

Create individual invocations to each trickster deity. This can be in the form of a poem or some other text that you recite at your altar. Start by thinking about what represents each one and how he/she influences your life already, and give thanks for this. If you're feeling creative, set your poem to music or develop a chant. Stretching your imagination in this way not only lifts the spirits, but also can help to unleash hidden talents.

80

CHAPTER FOUR

Traditional

Tricksters 81

Tricksters live on in our imagination because they're an inherent part of the oral tradition. They come to life in stories and legends that have been passed on through the ages. They are characters that we grew up with, hapless and unpredictable heroes who featured in fireside stories. They are the rascals who captured our hearts and minds when we were children, and the characters we were warned about through cautionary tales. The trickster is an essential part of traditional storytelling. His archetype is a key building block in universal narratives, because we can identify with some part of his or her personality. In addition, when you introduce the trickster element to a story, you give the story wings. You're opening the narrative structure to the unknown and throwing in a curveball, and that allows the tale to grow. It allows us to ask questions. What if? What happens now? How can this be resolved?

Traditional tricksters have all the same qualities as the other tricksters we have already learned about. The only difference is that their tales tend to impart lessons. The meaning is evident and easy to understand. The pattern and structure of the story are simple to follow, and take nothing away from the central trickster character and his dilemma. Unlike other tricksters, who can appear frightening and somewhat cruel, these characters err on the side of recklessness. They're lazy and immature—fools about to embark on a personal journey with much to learn. Their apparent innocence makes them likable and means that we engage with the story to form a deeper understanding of the core meaning. Traditional tricksters are learning tools and great fun to work with. They help us recognize the power of words and the importance of narrative, and how, in effect, we create the story of our lives every day. They show us how to reach inside and embrace trickster energy in a positive, proactive way.

JACK

One of the most famous archetypes in English folklore, Jack crops up in tales, rhymes, and stories as the lazy, hapless hero. Think Jack and the Beanstalk, known for his infamous giant-killing skill, Jack Sprat, who ate no fat, Jack-o'-Lantern, and prickly Jack Frost, to name just a few. A trickster and a fool, he ultimately grows in wit and charm and saves the day. The name Jack was first recorded in the thirteenth century, but it has gone on to represent everyman in the oral tradition. For this reason, there's something vulnerable and appealing about Jack. We can identify with his failings, because, like Jack, we've made mistakes along the way. This type of trickster has luck on his side, and often falls in the way of good fortune. Most Jack tales start with him as a poor and often silly young boy with grand ideas, who sets out on a quest to find his fortune and place in the world. Usually by magical means, Jack encounters help, and through a series of trials and tricks he finds his situation vastly improved. Again, we can identify with this kind of quest, because we see something of our own destiny in the narrative. Jack tales often involve kings who set impossible challenges, but trickster Jack has luck and arrogance on his side, and the combination brings him success. Jack can also refer to the character Jack in the Green, who usually pops up during May Day celebrations, adorned in flowers and greenery.

RITUAL

Attract prosperity and good fortune by tapping into Jack's vibrant energy. Take a green candle and a quartz crystal point, and carve a symbol representing success—such as a star or sun—into the wax. Light the candle. Gather a bunch of flowers and weave the stems together to make a small garland or wreath. Place the candle in the center of the circle of flowers, and think about what good fortune would mean to you. If you were successful, how would you live and what would you do? Imagine watching a movie of yourself in the future. See yourself surrounded by all the things you want, living the perfect life. You have achieved your dreams, and, like Jack, you've been successful in your quest. Let the candle burn down and place the garland of flowers somewhere prominent, so that every time you see it you think about a successful future.

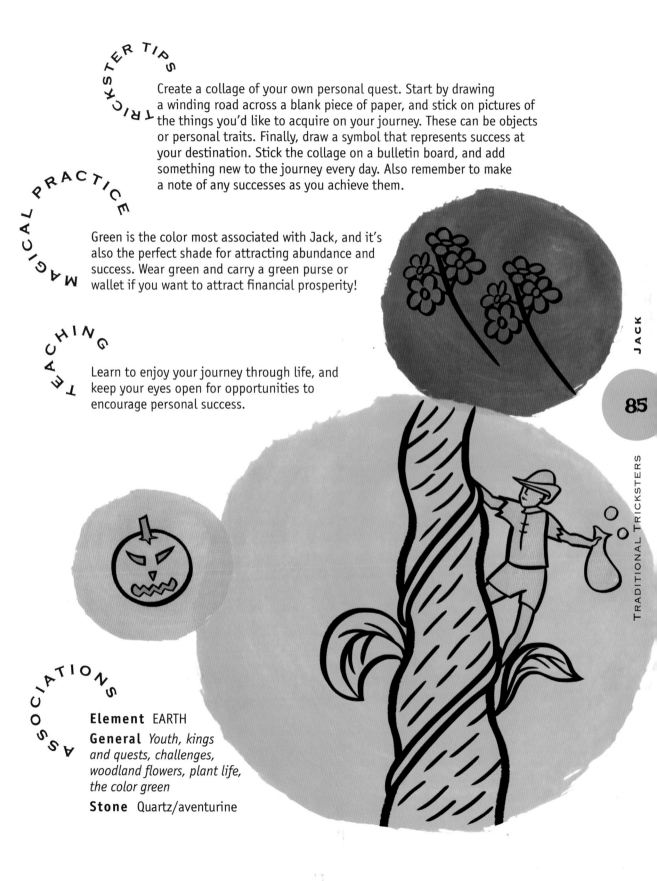

TRICKSTER TIPS

Create a collage of your own personal quest. Start by drawing a winding road across a blank piece of paper, and stick on pictures of the things you'd like to acquire on your journey. These can be objects or personal traits. Finally, draw a symbol that represents success at your destination. Stick the collage on a bulletin board, and add something new to the journey every day. Also remember to make a note of any successes as you achieve them.

MAGICAL PRACTICE

Green is the color most associated with Jack, and it's also the perfect shade for attracting abundance and success. Wear green and carry a green purse or wallet if you want to attract financial prosperity!

TEACHING

Learn to enjoy your journey through life, and keep your eyes open for opportunities to encourage personal success.

85

ASSOCIATIONS

Element EARTH
General *Youth, kings and quests, challenges, woodland flowers, plant life, the color green*
Stone Quartz/aventurine

Immortalized in Shakespeare's play *A Midsummer Night's Dream*, Puck is a mercurial character, a trickster and an imp, a fairy with a mischievous spirit. He's also commonly known as Robin Goodfellow, the spirit of the woods. In Welsh his name is Pwca, and in Irish Phouka or Pooka. He's an important

PUCK

part of English folklore, featuring in many tales and guises. It's hard to pin down his appearance; in some stories he's small and hairy, in others a silver-skinned elf, and he can also appear as an old man or even an animal. A master at transformation, Puck uses this to his advantage. As Robin Goodfellow, he's a hobgoblin who enjoys playing tricks on weary travelers, leading them a merry dance through the woods. He's also similar to the house fairy known as a brownie, and will often do jobs around the house in return for a saucer of milk or cream, or a taste of butter. Puck is often linked to the Devil. The medieval word pouk means "devil" and there's a dark side to this fey spirit, but in most tales he's depicted as cheeky and troublesome, a practical joker with magical powers. In addition to his enchantments, Puck is expert at cleaning and needlework.

TEACHING

Be aware of the wonder, joy, and beauty of the world around you, and take a lighter approach to life.

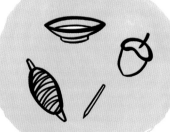

RITUAL

Attract good fortune and invite joy into your world with this ritual. Find an acorn and pierce a hole through the center with a needle. Loop red or gold thread through the acorn so that it hangs like a pendant. Light a yellow candle and spend a few minutes clearing your mind of any worries, then hold the acorn out in front of you and let it swing gently, like a pendulum. As it moves back and forth, think of the ticking of the clock and how every minute is precious. Say, "Spritely Puck with your spirit bright, help my heart be loving and light. With these words I call upon Puck. Bless me with an abundance of luck!" Repeat the chant over and over as the pendulum swings, until you feel relaxed and positive. When you're ready, tie the acorn pendant around your neck or wrist as a charm to attract good fortune.

MAGICAL PRACTICE

Puck enjoys life. He has fun, plays music, and celebrates the joy in every moment. Follow suit by playing your favorite song, having a sing-along, and dancing to the beat. Let yourself get lost in the moment, and imagine you're on stage giving the performance of your life!

TRICKSTER TIPS

Before important events, meetings, or competitions, dip your ritual acorn in powdered nutmeg and roll it over the palms of both hands while repeating the ritual chant. Nutmeg is associated with success in gambling, and can bring luck at just the right time.

ASSOCIATIONS

Element AIR/EARTH
General *Woods, trees (particularly oak and ash), sewing and needlework, music*
Stone Citrine/peridot

A magician and trickster,
Gwydion features in Welsh mythology.
He's considered a hero, and his exploits are
recounted in the Welsh Triads, the Book of Taliesin and
the Fourth Branch of the Mabinogi, eleven folk tales that
draw on Celtic symbolism. His name means "born of trees," and
he's closely associated with the natural world. His two favorite
tricks were to change shape and to turn people into animals.
Gwydion is most famous for being a surrogate father to his nephew
Lleu, whom he brings up from a baby. In one tale he creates the perfect
wife for Lleu out of flowers. Her name is Blodeuwedd, and she is an
incredibly beautiful flower maiden, but her beauty is only on the surface,
and she turns out to be a liar and a cheat. When Gwydion realizes her
true nature, he turns her into an owl. Powerful and wise, Gwydion
earned his stripes the hard way and performed many reckless

GWYDION (GWID-ee-on)

acts during his journey into
manhood; it's even thought that April Fools' Day originated
in the tricks he played in his early years. In some tales
he's thought of as a sky god, and associated with
the arts and creativity.

RITUAL

Stand tall and strong and cast away past mistakes with this easy ritual. If possible,
perform it outside beneath an oak tree. Stand with your feet hip-width apart, your
shoulders relaxed, and you arms at your sides. Visualize roots stretching from the
soles of your feet deep into the earth, like those of a tree. Raise your arms and
imagine they're branches stretching out into the world. Think of any mistakes or
behavior that you'd like to let go of, and see them as leaves on your branches.
Imagine watching them turn golden brown and fall to the ground, to be absorbed
by the earth. Say, "I cast away my former sins, the things I've done I'd like to
change. I release the pain, the stress, and fear, I start again, right now, right here."
Feel the roots beneath your feet feeding you with positive energy, and imagine this
stream of energy passing up through your spine and out at the top of your head.
Relax and spend a few minutes shaking your limbs to help the energy circulate.

TEACHING

Believe in yourself and use your imagination when you need prosperity and financial assistance, or to increase your creativity.

MAGICAL PRACTICE

If you're in need of cash fast, place a piece of carnelian in your purse and make a wish for abundance. Picture a red dragon showering you with gold coins as you do so.

TRICKSTER TIPS

Place the coins from the ritual in a pot and leave it beside the dragon image or figurine. Every day, add a coin to the pot while repeating the magical chant. After a month, you'll have amassed a stash of cash and also sent a powerful message to the universe, increasing your money vibration.

ASSOCIATIONS

Element FIRE
General *Horses, dragons, gold and silver coins, wheat, grain*
Stone Garnet/carnelian

Hitar Petar is a character from Bulgarian folklore. His name translates as Sly Peter, and he was known for his clever pranks and exploits. An antagonist of the rich, he often went head to head with clerics and noblemen, which

HITAR PETAR (HIT-ar PE-tar)

made him a favorite hero of the poor. His wily temperament served him well in many tricky situations. For example, one tale tells how one evening he saw a local judge staggering around drunk. The judge tossed his leather coat down at the side of the road, thinking he would pick it up later, but Peter grabbed the coat and put it on. The next day the judge sent one of his servants to look for the person who had stolen his coat. When the servant saw Peter, he took him to face the judge. Peter, knowing the coat belonged to the judge, explained that he'd seen it on the back of a drunk and disorderly layabout, and that he was wearing it in order to return it to him. He then asked the judge, with a crafty wink, if he knew who this reprobate was, putting the judge in an uncomfortable position and making him unable to own up to the truth! Hitar Petar is associated with April Fools' Day because of his ability to be a joker.

RITUAL

This ritual will help you to be more spontaneous and think on your feet. Steep a sprig of fresh rosemary in a cup of hot water for five minutes, then remove the rosemary and add a squeeze of fresh lemon. Sip the brew slowly while asking Hitar Petar to open your heart and mind. If you have a particular problem or situation that you need help with, focus on it as you drink. When you've finished, take the Joker from a pack of playing cards, place the sprig of rosemary over the card, and wrap it in black silk, or, if you have a leather charm bag, place it inside. Say, "I ask Sly Peter with this ditty, to activate my charm and make me witty. Upon my feet I think and act, with charm, good humor, diplomacy, and tact." Keep the card and sprig of rosemary with you as a charm to encourage an active mind, and sleep with it under your pillow for inspiring dreams!

TEACHING

Be less judgmental of yourself and others. Use your quick wit and resourceful mind if you're in a tight spot or need to impress.

MAGICAL PRACTICE

Hitar Petar is good with witty retorts. Sharpen your mind by practicing some tongue twisters, such as "Peter Piper picked a peck of pickled peppers. A peck of pickled peppers Peter Piper picked. If Peter Piper picked a peck of pickled peppers, where's the peck of pickled peppers that Peter Piper picked?"

TRICKSTER TIPS

Use the Joker from your charm in a fun prediction game. Extract the ace from every suit and mix the four cards with the Joker. Without looking at the cards, close your eyes and ask Sly Peter to reveal the theme of the day. Choose a card and turn it over. If it's hearts, your day will be blessed with love; if it's diamonds, money; if you pick clubs, business dealings are important; and if you choose spades, it's a day of action. If you pick the Joker, expect the unexpected!

ASSOCIATIONS

Element EARTH

General *April 1, Joker playing card, coat, cloak*

Stone Agate

These tricksters from Japanese folklore are fiery fox spirits with attitude! They have the ability to shape-shift into human form, often appearing as beautiful young women or as older men, but they gain this power only once they've lived as a fox for 100 years.

KITSUNE (kit-soo-ni)

With up to nine tails, it's thought that the kitsune carries its power in its tail. It has more than one in order to conceal this, and anyone who wants to steal its power and life must cut off all of them. When a kitsune spirit gains its ninth tail, its fur turns white or gold. These wise, clever tricksters have supernatural powers, and the ability to know what is happening anywhere in the world. They can be benevolent and helpful or mischievous, playing tricks on the unsuspecting and hiding things from humans. They have a frivolous attitude, flitting from one thing to another. It's thought that when a kitsune changes into human form, it can sometimes forget to hide its tail, or it might even appear with fox-like features and a fine coating of fur. Kitsunes love their freedom, and they hate to be caged or controlled. They have the ability to become invisible, breathe fire and lightning, and create powerful illusions. The more powerful the kitsune, the more impressive its feats, and some are believed to be able to change into other things entirely, such as trees or even the moon.

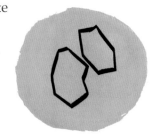

RITUAL

Create a wish box to help you fulfill your heart's desire, and dedicate it to the kitsune. Start with a cardboard carton and decorate the outside with images of foxes, the moon, and shades of red and gold. You might want to use ribbons or glitter to make it vibrant and appealing. Fill the carton with items associated with these trickster spirits—perhaps nine pieces of red string to symbolize their nine tails, a piece of amber, images of foxes, a lump of fool's gold, and so on. Finish by writing a dedication to the kitsune, such as, "I embrace the flow of kitsune magic into my life. I celebrate my freedom and my ability to go with the flow. I dedicate this wish box to the kitsune as a thank you for their influence every day." Light a candle while saying the dedication out loud. Every day write down a quotation, a wish, or something that you'd like to attract more of into your life—"wealth," "freedom," or "fun," for example—place it in the box and repeat the affirmation.

TEACHING

Be spontaneous and free, and embrace your individuality and your unique gifts, to find your place in the world or strike out on your own.

MAGICAL PRACTICE

To get things moving in your life, light a red or gold candle on an evening when the moon is waxing (getting bigger). Gaze at the flame and ask the kitsune to bless you with swift action and success!

TRICKSTER TIPS

Take your wish box a step further and include a journal in which you can chart your thoughts, feelings, and successes. If you notice some trickster magic at work in your life, make a note of it and give thanks to the playful kitsune.

ASSOCIATIONS

Element FIRE

General *Fire, lightning, the moon, the number 9, the colors red and gold*

Stone Fool's gold (iron pyrite)/amber

The hero twins feature in one of
the oldest Mayan myths to be preserved.
There are many versions of this first story, but the
essence of the tale is that the twins' father and uncle were
summoned to the underworld, where they were sacrificed before
the boys were born. The twins made it their mission to avenge their
father's death, and finally defeated the lords of the underworld in a ball

MAYAN HERO TWINS

game! The twins performed many exploits, some of which involved trickery and deceit. They killed a bird demon and its two sons, and turned their half-brothers into the Howler Monkey gods. The culmination of their adventures was when they transformed themselves into the sun and the moon. This transformation represented the beginning of a new age in Mayan mythology. In early images and ceramics, the twins appear quite different—one has black spots on his face and is associated with death, and the other, often called "the war twin," looks almost jaguar-like with patches of fur and whiskers.

Quick-thinking and nimble on their feet, the hero twins didn't realize they could play ball until a chance encounter with a rat. The rat revealed that both their father and their uncle were skilled at ball games, and that they had inherited this talent.

RITUAL

Embrace the power of the Hero Twins and feel energized and ready for action with this easy ritual. Take an orange candle to represent the sun and a white candle to represent the moon. Place them side by side and light them. If you have a particular problem on your mind, write it down on a piece of paper and place it between the two candles. Say, "By the power of two, both light and dark, bring clarity, vision, and an energizing spark! By the power of the hero twins, and two sides of the story, illuminate my life with divine joy and glory." Pass the paper through both flames, setting it alight. Scatter the ashes of the paper outdoors and let the candles burn down. As you do so, imagine an orb like the sun in your chest, filling you with warmth, and visualize the moon above you, bathing you in white light.

TEACHING

Work with others to achieve your goals. Remember that there are two sides to every story.

MAGICAL PRACTICE

If you want to tap into the magic of the Mayan Hero Twins, play ball. Simply throwing a tennis ball at the wall or bouncing it off the floor will help to focus your mind. Visualize the goal you'd like to achieve, and, as the ball hits its target, imagine you've achieved your dream!

TRICKSTER TIPS

Perform the ritual twice on the same day, first by the light of the sun in the morning, and then again in the evening when the moon is in the sky. Repeating the ritual will reinforce the dual power of the twins, and bring twice the clarity and energy!

ASSOCIATIONS

Element AIR/EARTH
General *Ball games, sport, the sun, the moon, jaguars*
Stone Moonstone

Taking It Further

Traditional tricksters come in many forms, and various patterns and symbols are repeated, particularly in the narrative structure. These characters resonate with us on a subconscious level. If you're drawn to these beings, dig a little deeper and discover how to work with their powerful symbols.

Repetition is key in most tales of traditional tricksters, and it is highly effective when you are trying to instigate positive change. Try using it with an affirmation that embraces trickster magic. For example, throughout the day, every time you see your reflection, say (out loud or in your head), "I embrace the trickster spirit in me. I step forward with boundless energy!"

Have a go at some oral storytelling. Get a group of friends together and establish an informal storytelling circle, where everyone takes a turn at telling a traditional tale. Choose a story that features your favorite traditional trickster. This will help you tap into the trickster's energy, and also give your creativity a boost.

Fairy tales are traditional. They are littered with trickster characters, and many are based on old folk tales. Imagine your life is a fairy tale and introduce an element of magic into the narrative. For example, if you're looking for a new job, see yourself stumbling on a door that leads to a new way of life and career. Write the story and give yourself a happy, fairy-tale ending, then read it every day to reinforce a positive message and outcome.

CHAPTER FIVE

Modern
Tricksters

103

We've all got something of the trickster about us. Even the most straightforward individual has the ability to surprise and to throw caution to the wind. We are all motivated by the same urges; we all have hopes, dreams, and dark desires. We have flights of fancy and humorous thoughts, and, let's be honest, we can also succumb to devilish deeds and dark emotions. What limits these things is the way we choose to behave. Our background and morals come into play, and in most cases we consider the outcome of our actions. But despite all this we love a good trickster. We enjoy seeing tricksters in action, because we can identify with their true nature. It lives inside of us and it's fun to see that side of human nature being embraced. We might not want to go down that road ourselves, for fear of the repercussions, but we get to live out these fantasies through watching and reading about their exploits. That is why this archetype is still very much alive and well today. We see trickster characters all the time in the media, on television, in movies, and in the books we read. They may be modern versions of the old tales, but they have the same traits, the same unpredictable energy that is so addictive.

Consider adrenalin junkies. They get their highs from joining in adventurous and often dangerous activities; they enjoy stepping outside of their comfort zone, if only for a short time, because the unknown gives them a thrill. These characters are embracing their trickster spirit. You could even say they're the modern version of old wily Coyote or Brer Rabbit. Think about the people you know. It's likely that there will be one trickster in the bunch, one character who embraces that energy and, as such, has become a focal point of the group. We often use "the life and soul of the party" to describe these individuals, but it might be more correct to say that they're tapping into their inner trickster. This chapter looks at modern tricksters in all their guises. Just because they're of this world, that doesn't mean they're any less powerful. These characters, most of whom grace the silver screen, have been created to fulfill a need for this kind of magical energy. Working with them can bring about a shift in the way you think, act, and see the world, while giving you a super-cool air of confidence!

This lovable rascal from the *Pirates of the Caribbean* movies is the personification of a trickster. Outlandish and frivolous, and seeming to care only about himself, Jack is a wayward individual. His actions, mostly self-

CAPTAIN JACK SPARROW

serving, often result in him saving the day even if that wasn't his intention. A complex character, like Coyote, you never know what he's thinking or how he's going to react. This unpredictability is key to the spirit of the trickster. There's also a bawdiness about this pirate that fits in nicely with Coyote's vulgar nature. In the third movie, Jack and Captain Barbossa compete to find out who has the largest telescope. Phallic innuendo is rife, and a similar coarse humor can be found in some of the earliest Native American tales of Coyote's exploits. A weaver of words and riddles, Jack knows how to turn up the charm, as he states quite clearly: "I'm dishonest, and a dishonest man you can always trust to be dishonest. Honestly." Jack is also a survivor. As he says to Captain Barbossa, after being abandoned on an island in the middle of nowhere, "When you marooned me on that godforsaken spit of land, you forgot one very important thing, mate: I'm Captain Jack Sparrow."

RITUAL

Fulfill your ambitions and aim for career success by tapping into some of Jack's mystic magic. Choose a night when the moon is a crescent and waxing (getting larger). Place a coin in the bottom of a bowl of water, and leave it on a window ledge in the light of the moon. On a piece of paper, write down the ambition you'd like to fulfill, such as "I will run my own successful business." Fold the paper and place it underneath the bowl of water. Spend a few minutes breathing deeply, then look up at the moon and say, "As I navigate this Earth, my wishes manifest. The treasure that I seek is mine, for I am blessed." Finally, visualize yourself opening a treasure chest. Inside it, you see a vision of yourself achieving your ambition. Imagine how you'll feel when this happens, and enjoy those happy emotions. The following morning, remove the coin from the bowl and bury it outdoors with the paper. Repeat the affirmation.

MAGICAL PRACTICE

Pirates are opportunists. They make their own luck. Manifest good fortune by making a chest of treasures. Fill a box with beads, jewels, stones, photos, and pictures of all the things you love and want in your life. Add to it every week to keep the energy of abundance flowing!

TEACHING

No matter what life throws at you, you can overcome it and succeed if you use your intuition. Be determined and tenacious and you can achieve anything.

TRICKSTER TIPS

Use the treasure-chest visualization every morning to project an image of how you'd like things to go that day. When you open the chest, imagine you're bathed in golden light, as you see the vision of your perfect day unfolding. Say, "Whatever comes my way, I enjoy this day!"

ASSOCIATIONS

Element WATER

General *Sparrows (or other small flying birds), the crescent moon, string, beads, gold coins, compasses, the sea*

Stone Pearl

This lovable rascal is accustomed to getting himself into and out of trouble. First appearing on our screens in 1940 in the short *A Wild Hare*,

BUGS BUNNY

he went on to feature in a number of animated movies, most famously the Looney Tunes series and the television series Merrie Melodies (1990). This gray rabbit, with a broad American drawl and the famous catchphrase "Eh … What's up, Doc?" is a trickster with a flippant attitude. Like Anansi, the spider of African folklore, he uses other people's stupidity to his advantage, outsmarting them in an instant. A master of disguise, he shares the common trickster shape-shifting theme, but instead of transforming his shape, he simply impersonates different characters, including the rich and famous. He also enjoys dressing in drag. Not afraid of causing offence, and with a wicked sense of fun, Bugs Bunny is probably one of the most likable fictional tricksters. With a confident swagger, Bugs has many talents, including singing, which he does in most of his movie roles. He's also partial to chomping on a carrot while contemplating his next plan of attack! Cool and audacious, Bugs is hard to pin down, as most of his opponents, including Daffy Duck, Porky Pig, and Elmer Fudd, soon realize.

RITUAL

Get Bugs Bunny Zen and learn how to chill when the going gets tough. Although Bugs Bunny is an animated character, his attitude can teach us a great deal, particularly during stressful periods. His favorite stance usually involved him folding his arms while repeating some witty phrase. When you feel under attack, follow Bug Bunny's lead. Take a deep breath, smile confidently, and cross your arms in front of your chest. This protective action acts like a shield to the heart. Visualize an orange glow in the center of your chest, like the embers of a fire, and feel the warmth spread throughout your body. Now uncross your arms, stand tall, and relax your shoulders. Imagine a thread attached to the top of your head, and feel it pulling slightly and lengthening your spine. In your mind repeat the words "I can do this!"

TRICKSTER TIPS

Rabbits make a brilliant animal totem. They're fast and clever, and they channel their fear to give them extra oomph when facing a predator. Take a tip from them and face your fears every day. Whenever you feel challenged, repeat the affirmation from the ritual—"I can do this!"—and stand tall.

MAGICAL PRACTICE

Bugs knew the value of chomping on a carrot. This vibrant vegetable packs a powerful punch when combined with three celery sticks and an apple. Juice the lot, and drink while visualizing a vibrant, super-lean version of yourself under the spotlight.

TEACHING

Increase your personal magnetism to attract success. Learn to believe in yourself, and see the humorous side if things don't go your way.

ASSOCIATIONS

Element EARTH
General *Hares, rabbits, carrots, stars, singing*
Stone Diamond/amber

This trickster character started life as the Joker in a pack of cards, and was based on the original court jesters who would entertain nobility. Playing pranks

THE JOKER

and tricks, and acting the fool, these characters were ridiculed for their antics, which were usually the focus of any event. Dressed in red and yellow, and with bells dangling from their hats, they looked silly, but that was all part of their carefully planned performance. Also akin to the Fool tarot card, the Joker represented the naive idiot stepping out into the world without a care. But soon he developed a reputation, and he went from folklore to film as a notorious villain in the Batman movies. Cunning and cruel, this Joker liked to speak in riddles, wearing a painted-on goofy smile rather like a clown's, so that it was hard to read his true expression. A master of deception, this trickster is unpredictable and will do anything to get attention, rather like his court jester counterpart.

RITUAL

Open yourself up to a world of opportunity and some exciting new adventures with this easy ritual. Take the Joker playing card from a pack and place it in front of you. Think about your own life and when you've captured the spirit of the Joker. Do you find it easy to laugh and have fun, or do you restrict yourself and avoid new opportunities? Hold the card in both hands and tear it in two while saying, "I cut the ties that bind me, the restrictions that lock me in. I am free to explore and have fun with absolutely everything!" Continue to tear up the card into ever-smaller pieces while repeating the affirmation. Finally, scoop all the pieces up and place them in a drawstring pouch or bag as a charm to attract new adventures and opportunities into your life.

To clear the way for new opportunities, go from room to room in your home ringing a handbell. Imagine you're sweeping through each space like a refreshing breeze, clearing out negative energy and clutter.

MAGICAL PRACTICE

Make getting ready in the morning a magical experience by tapping into some Joker energy. As you do the dishes or bathe, apply makeup, or style your hair, imagine you're donning a mask that says, "I'm here and ready for the world!" Repeat this affirmation as you look at your reflection in the mirror, then smile your biggest smile!

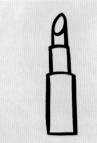

TEACHING

Make an impression and get noticed by those in power by letting your enthusiasm shine through.

111

ASSOCIATIONS

Element AIR/FIRE

General *Bells, hats, the colors red and yellow, lipstick, Joker playing card, Fool tarot card*

Stone Topaz

Popular around the world,
the super-smooth and slinky Pink
Panther first glided on to our screens in 1964 in a
short animated movie, *The Pink Phink*. In it, we see the
Pink Panther harassing a little man to paint his blue house
pink. In the early days, the Pink Panther was generally silent,
although that didn't detract from the narrative. Viewers would
observe the pantomime style of the story, with lots of creative, visual

THE PINK PANTHER

puns, almost always featuring the panther. He appeared very briefly in his
earlier incarnation during the opening titles of the feature film *The Pink
Panther* (1963), starring Peter Sellars, and set the tone of the story that
would follow. In later movies and animations the character gained a
voice as suave and debonair as the Panther himself. Adept at the art of
cool, the Pink Panther oozes confidence and charm. He doesn't shy
away from trouble or conflict, but is instead at the heart of the
action. Very rarely alarmed, he remains unfazed even when
faced with sudden peril. He is an example of one of the
slyest tricksters, and, like his traditional
counterparts, manages to get away with
things by putting on an act.

RITUAL

Cats are agile and very flexible, able to squeeze into and out of small spaces, just like the Pink
Panther who slips easily into and out of trouble. If you need to remain cool, calm, and collected,
tap into some Pink Panther magic with this ritual. Stand with your feet hip-width apart and your
shoulders relaxed. Breathe deeply in and bend forward from the hips with your arms stretched
out in front of you. Feel the stretch across your back and the back of your calves. Now rise up
from the waist so your arms are pointing to the ceiling, and gently bend backward as you breathe
out. Repeat several times, until your muscles feel loose and relaxed. Finish by imagining that
you have a cat's eye in the center of your forehead. As it opens, you become aware of everything
around you, all the sights, sounds, smells, and feelings. Say, "Like a cat flexing its toes, my
inner strength and presence grows, an inner core of perfect peace, as all my stress I now
release." The combination of stretching and visualization works both inner and outer muscles,
strengthening your core and improving flexibility, both physical and mental.

TEACHING

Remain calm in a crisis, exude charm in any situation, and increase your confidence in yourself.

MAGICAL PRACTICE

Pink is the color of love, and the Pink Panther has had his share of admiration over the years. Increase your personal magnetism by wearing a splash of pink, particularly near your face. Go for a pink scarf or tie, or a slick of pink lipstick. Increase the attraction by carrying a piece of rose quartz in your pocket.

TRICKSTER TIPS

Activate your cat's eye at any point during the day when you need clarity or to tap into your intuition. Imagine this big golden eye acting as a radar, picking up on thoughts and feelings, and attracting positive energy toward you.

ASSOCIATIONS

Element AIR
General *The color pink, cats, anything as dazzling as glitter or crystals*
Stone Diamond/rose quartz

PETER PAN

When Disney released its animated motion picture *Peter Pan* in 1953, it took the spirit of Pan the trickster deity and placed it in the body of a young boy in the film, adapting the original character created by J. M. Barrie. Like Pan, he dressed in green and had pointy ears and magical powers, one of which was the ability to fly. His youthful exuberance, as with many of the traditional tricksters, can be seen as naive folly, and—also like his trickster counterparts—Peter has big ideas that don't always go to plan. An accessible trickster watered down for children to enjoy, he nevertheless still embodies many characteristics of this archetype and has an energy that we can identify with. With his tales of Neverland, the magical world that exists beyond the second star on the right, Peter is a dreamer. He urges us to use our imagination and have fun. His army of companions, the Lost Boys, are rebellious souls who understand his spontaneous nature. In the Steven Spielberg movie *Hook* (1991), actor Robin Williams takes Peter to another level. As a grown-up with responsibilities, he's lost his sense of fun and needs to find his inner child to save the day—and himself. In one line, he says, "To die will be an awfully big adventure." This captures the essence of this trickster character, an eternal optimist, sometimes foolish, but always looking for adventure.

RITUAL

Dedicate your yard to Peter Pan, or, if you don't have the outdoor space, make a window box. Include lots of color and greenery, and decorate it with fairy lights. Hang wind chimes from trees or windows. Once you've set aside a space, however small, spend some time every day tending to it. Use it as a place to contemplate dreams and wishes. Take a small bell into the area and declare your dreams like a town crier, ringing the bell after every wish to attract the attention of the universe. Also write down any wishes and bury them in the earth.

TRICKSTER TIPS

Engage your imagination and consider what your perfect Neverland would be like. How would it look and how would you spend your days there? Are there any things that you'd do that you can incorporate into your daily routine? For example, if you'd spend your time singing and dancing, perhaps you could take up a dance class, or join a choir.

MAGICAL PRACTICE

Renew your enthusiasm for life and give your energy levels a boost by spending some time outdoors. Go for a walk in the park, or simply spend time foraging in your yard. Get to grips with the greenery and explore. Imagine you're seeing things for the first time. Make a note either physically or in your head of the things that stand out. Draw, describe, and let the landscape inspire you!

TEACHING

Embrace your inner child to revive your enthusiasm for life, find excitement, or work a change in any area.

ASSOCIATIONS

Element AIR
General *Pipes or flute, fairies, lanterns, flight, bells, the forest, the color green*
Stone Aventurine

The Doctor is the main fictional character in a long-running British science-fiction series. He's the epitome of the trickster, in that he regenerates and changes

DOCTOR WHO

shape and guise every so often. This transformation is not dissimilar to the shape-shifting antics of Coyote and his animal cousins. So far the Doctor has been portrayed by twelve different actors, all of whom have a slightly different take on the character. That is because the doctor is mercurial, and, like all the tricksters before him, has different sides to his personality. Another common trickster trait is his wit and ingenuity. In every narrative he finds himself in a tight spot, often because of his curious spirit. He uses his mind rather than force to save the day, even when faced with fierce opposition. Like Loki and other trickster deities, his power is in his creative charm, although he also manages to have a degree of luck on his side. He usually travels with a companion, someone with a grounding influence who can help him channel his erratic energy for the good of others. He is sometimes irresponsible and acts with what seems like little thought, but the Doctor's magic is in his spontaneous nature. Each Doctor has his own quirky sense of style, with certain items associated solely with that persona—for example, Tom Baker's long multicolored scarf and Matt Smith's bow tie.

RITUAL

This ritual will get you firing on all cylinders and ready to take on the world! Stand underneath the blanket of the sky and look up at the stars. Even if you can't see them, they're there. Now imagine extending your spirit—the core energy inside of you—upward. Imagine the subconscious part of your mind soaring out of the top of your head, like a flash of white light. Feel this presence flying up to the stars. This is your spiritual essence, so you are fully aware of what is happening and can feel and see the night sky around you. Go beyond the clouds, up into the universe, and imagine you can see the Earth, a tiny globe, below you. Feel the immense magic of space around you, and the vastness of the universe. Take a deep breath in and imagine filling your heart with this sense of power. Say, "I am the universe and the universe is me!" Now see yourself slowly returning to Earth, traveling back down past the stars, toward the planet, until eventually you slide neatly back into your physical body. Give your arms and legs a shake. You should feel energized and invigorated.

MAGICAL PRACTICE

Take inspiration from the Doctor's quirky sense of style and introduce a unique accessory into your everyday wear to say something about your personality. For example, you may want to wear a brooch in the shape of a star for success and luck, or a brightly colored hat to represent joy and energy. Whatever you pick, make sure you associate it with a positive attribute, so that whenever you wear it, it becomes your personal armor.

TEACHING

See things from a different perspective to engage your creative mind, express your unique voice, and move forward with flair.

TRICKSTER TIPS

You don't have to restrict the ritual to an evening. You can do it anytime and anywhere. Just imagine leaving your body and soaring up into the heavens. This is the perfect exercise to do before a presentation or important meeting, as it gives both confidence and an energy boost!

ASSOCIATIONS

Element ALL ELEMENTS (EARTH/AIR/FIRE/WATER)

General *Tardis, space, infinity, stars, items specific to each Doctor*

Stone Meteor stone/granite

The character of Jack Frost appears in the Disney movie *The Santa Clause 3: The Escape Clause* (2006). Jack is devilish, charming, and incredibly sly in his plans to overthrow Santa. In the movie he plays countless tricks, including disguising the North Pole as Canada and fooling the head elf into revealing Santa's treasured secret, the "escape clause." He is based on the character from

JACK FROST

myth and legend who represents cold, icy weather. It's thought that his origins are in a Norse tale about a boy called Jokul Frosti ("Icicle Frost"), who spent his nights going from window to window painting beautiful icicle patterns. In folklore, Jack Frost is depicted as an elf-like character with bluish skin and the ability to freeze anything he touches. Wherever he goes, he brings wintry weather. In Russia there are similar stories about a Father Frost, both harsh and kind in nature, depending on his mood and how people treat him. The Jack Frost who features in movies and books today is a mercurial character; like the Norse god Loki, he is changeable, sometimes good, sometimes bad. In *The Santa Clause 3* he starts with evil plans, but then has a change of heart. He delights in causing mayhem, as he himself explains: "Did you just accuse me of being skillful and delicious? Guilty as charged!" Just like the mythic character Jack Frost, he brings the icy wind of change into our lives.

RITUAL

The best way to tap into Jack's invigorating power is to use the element of water. This ritual is best performed in the evening when the moon is waxing (getting bigger). Light white and blue candles to represent Jack, and leave them burning in your bathroom. Start by standing beneath a warm shower. Think about all the things you'd like to let go of, and ways in which you'd like to improve yourself and your life. When you're ready, flick the temperature to cold for just a few seconds or, if you prefer, pour a bowl of cold water over your head. Feel the icy chill sending a wave of energy through your body and renewing your strength and vigor. Say, "By the magic of Jack Frost, that which is bad is lost. That which is good returns to me, I am renewed, alive and free!" Increase the temperature again and enjoy the feeling of the warm water pouring over you and cleansing your body.

TEACHING

Let go of bad emotions in order to start afresh, heal your heart, and attract new love.

MAGICAL PRACTICE

Dedicate your bathroom to Jack Frost by incorporating lots of blue, white, and silver decoration. Include candles, shells, and icicle patterns, and leave clusters of quartz and aquamarine in a dish by the sink. Every time you wash your hands, hold a crystal afterward and make a wish!

TRICKSTER TIPS

Perform the ritual when washing your hair in the morning, for an instant energy fix. Wait until the last rinse and use a bowl of iced water. After rinsing, massage your scalp briskly while imagining that you're stimulating and focusing the mind!

ASSOCIATIONS

Element WATER/AIR

General *Ice, snow, frost, water, the colors white and blue*

Stone Aquamarine/quartz

The mysterious candyman of
Roald Dahl's imagination appears in the
book *Charlie and the Chocolate Factory* (1964), and on
the silver screen portrayed by Gene Wilder and Johnny
Depp. Reclusive and quirky, this character is described by Dahl

WILLY WONKA

as like "a quick, clever
old squirrel from the
park." There's something strange about Wonka—he's hard to pin down.
Wilder's interpretation embodies the trickster spirit, being capricious and
changeable, warm and cruel at the same time. As the story unfolds, each child
who has won a tour of the chocolate factory reveals his or her true nature
(which isn't pleasant), and gets their just deserts. Charlie, however, the poor
boy accompanied by his grandfather, proves his mettle and becomes the
accidental hero of the day. Wonka, like many tricksters in history, tests the
children as a way of identifying their true worth. The book and the movies
use powerful imagery to get this message across, and
there's a strong element of fantasy to Wonka. Like a
magician, he has created an enchanting world filled
with chocolate rivers, Oompa-Loompas, and everlasting
gobstoppers. Wonka remains mercurial and inventive.
He's an example of a modern trickster with an
ingenious, playful spirit.

RITUAL

Ensure success with this enchanting ritual to promote action.
Imagine that, like Willy Wonka, you have a magical cane or wand.
If you have a cane or walking stick, use that, otherwise pick an
everyday object such as an umbrella or even a wooden spoon. Mark
out a circle in your family room by laying down a mat or using
crystals and stones to create the shape. Stand in the center of the
circle with your makeshift wand, and visualize an area of your life
that you'd like to improve. You might want to attract new love or
secure a pay rise, for instance. Now picture a symbol to represent
this area; for love you might think of a heart, and for money a pot
of gold coins. Hold the image in your mind and say, "What I see
I draw to me, I enhance this magically. I love life and it loves me.
What I see I draw to me!" Now point your wand in front of you and
imagine directing a dart of energy toward your goal. Repeat the ritual
once a week for maximum success!

TRICKSTER TIPS

To seal the ritual and reinforce to the universe the concept that you deserve a "reward," finish by eating a piece of your favorite chocolate or candy—just a small piece, to acknowledge that you are special and deserve success!

MAGICAL PRACTICE

Imagine you've been given a golden ticket that will allow you access to a bright new world. Each morning, you take your ticket and go off on an adventure. Look at the world through young eyes. Engage all your senses as you move through the day. Experience everything by touching, smelling, feeling, listening, and seeing. Each evening, describe your day in a journal entry. Again, use all the senses to make the description come to life.

ASSOCIATIONS

Element AIR
General *Chocolate, candy, golden tickets, canes, wands*
Stone Amethyst/gold

TEACHING

Introduce an element of fun into your life and learn to appreciate the joy around you. Look for and create beauty wherever you go.

Taking It Further

Modern tricksters have an edge. They're essentially the same as their traditional cousins, but at times they take things a step further. They make us laugh, they take center stage, and they can teach us how to be more confident in our own skin. If you want to delve deeper into their world, here are a few tips to get you started.

Get arty. Most of the tricksters in this chapter leap from animated screens and comic books. They're vibrant and over the top, and their actions are often exaggerated. To get to grips with this type of "animated" energy, have a go at creating your own comic-book characters. Start by thinking about yourself—if you were in a cartoon, what type of character would you be? Have fun creating something. If you feel really imaginative, you can include your favorite modern trickster, and come up with a basic tale or a picture to represent your adventures together. The secret to identifying with this type of trickster is to get a sense of who they are and what makes them so vibrant. By being creative and working with this medium, you'll instinctively feel more alive and colorful.

Movies feature in the
recounting of modern trickster tales, so
think of your life in terms of one. For example, if
you're encountering a problem at work, play it out in
your head as if you're watching events unfold on the big
screen. See yourself as the central character. When it gets to
the point of crisis, freeze the frame. Now substitute your
favorite trickster character for yourself. What would he or she
do? How would they handle this and turn it to their
advantage? See the movie reach a positive conclusion, then
repeat the exercise, putting yourself back into the frame.
Notice how this makes you feel. If you feel confident
and relaxed, hold on to these emotions and
replay them in your mind when
dealing with real events.

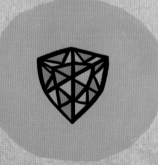

Modern tricksters tend to
use slapstick in their routines;
performance is part of what they do and
who they are. Enroll in a drama class or
have a go at stand-up comedy. If you prefer
something less challenging, come up with a
series of jokes and test them out on friends.
Get in touch with your inner joker and
learn to laugh at yourself and
with others.

THE TRICK IN THE TALE

It's hard to sum up the spirit of the trickster in a word. The archetype encompasses many different character traits, but the common thread is changeability–the ability to adapt and turn on a pinhead at the drop of a hat; to be good, bad, or indifferent. Tricksters are hard to pin down for this very reason. Just when you think you've got them sussed, they do something to make you wonder if you ever knew them at all! The bad guy becomes good and opens his heart; the ingenious hero suddenly has a lapse of concentration or throws caution to the wind, causing events to spiral out of control. But it's this capacity for change that makes the trickster such a crucial archetype. As humans, we can identify with this. We go through a series of changes in our life, both physical and emotional. We know that nothing stays the same forever, and we try to accept that. Tricksters blatantly throw this in our face with their exploits, saying, "Don't be afraid, come what may." That is why we adore them, because they're not scared—or, if they are, they don't show it. This bravado carries them through all sorts of adventures and precarious situations, and just when we think they're going to come to a sticky end, they come up trumps. That gives us hope.

We can learn a lot from the trickster. We learn about the unpredictable nature of life, and we learn about ourselves and how we handle things. We learn how to behave and how not to behave if we want to win friends and influence people; how to adapt and how to tap into the creative spirit. Most of all, tricksters open our eyes to the beauty and wonder of the world around us. They say, "Look around—it may be messy, but it's amazing too!" They show us that just because something isn't perfect, as we see it, that doesn't mean it's not perfect for us. And this is probably their most useful lesson. They break down barriers and perceptions, and challenge us to see things differently. In this they are sage and guru and the wisest of us all.

Another storyteller once recounted an experience she'd had with the trickster in its guise as Coyote. It's a story I remember because of its power and simplicity. She said that normally she'd avoided telling Coyote tales for fear that his influence would cause chaos in her life, but on one occasion she was urged to do so. She told a story that focused on the lighter, more helpful side of Coyote's nature. On the journey home she could feel herself nodding off at the wheel, but knew she was nearly there and was determined to get home before midnight. Suddenly she heard raucous laughter that seemed to be coming from the back seat. She checked her mirror, and there, staring back at her, was Coyote, looking every inch the man but wearing his coyote head and a cowboy hat. The sight made her jump, causing her to swerve just in time to avoid a huge truck coming toward her. She had obviously sunk into sleep and her car had drifted into another lane. If she hadn't had a vision of Coyote, she would certainly have come to a nasty end, or at least suffered a serious accident. An example of Coyote magic, perhaps? Definitely proof that working with tricksters can help us see things differently and open our eyes to the world.

Many things have happened to me during the writing of this book. There's certainly been trickster energy afoot! Some of these events have been unpleasant and frustrating, and some exciting, but mostly they've been unexpected. They've kept me on my toes. Although, like everyone, I'd like to avoid the trickier situations in life, I am happy that I don't know what's around the corner, because I now see every day as a new adventure. I know that I have the chance to write the narrative of my life, to be the trickster in my own tale, and to create a happy and fabulous ending. Whenever things appear to be up in the air, I ask myself what my favorite trickster would do, and I take note of my intuitive reaction. I take myself out of the situation and see it as a story unfolding, a story that I can change and improve upon. Rather than facing the future with fear, I open my heart and say, "Bring it on!" while imagining Coyote and his merry band of trickster friends doing a dance in my family room. I'm sure somewhere out there in the mystical "otherworld," that's exactly what's happening. If you're trying to find your way in the world, to start afresh, or simply to attract more joy into your life, throw your arms open and invite the trickster into your life. Let this book be your guide, or just follow your heart. If something has struck a chord with you while reading, pay attention. It's probably your trickster giving you a nudge, saying, "I'm here! Embrace the magic and go with the flow."

Remember, we all have an element of the trickster within us—it's what makes us human. So have fun working some trickster magic. I promise you won't be disappointed!

INDEX

A
Aengus 90–1
Africa 16–17, 70–1
African American tales 18
altars 66, 78, 79
Anansi the Spider 13,
  16–17
animal tricksters 9, 12–13
  Anansi the Spider 13,
    16–17
  Brer Rabbit 18–19
  Coyote 6, 14–15, 124–5
  Crow 6, 22–3
  Manabozho 24–5
  Monkey 26–7
  Raven 6, 13, 20–1
  Reynard the Fox 28–9
Appalachian Jack 36–7
April Fools' Day 88, 94
asserting yourself 69
aura 21, 25
Australian Aboriginal tales
  22, 42–3
Aztec deity 76–7

B
Bamapana 42–3
Bigmouth 92–3
birds
  Crow 6, 22–3
  feeding 67
  matin-taperê 48
  owl 50, 51
  Raven 6, 13, 20–1
  swans 90, 91
boundaries, pushing 42–3
Brazil 48
Brer Rabbit 18–19
Bugs Bunny 108–9
Bulgaria 94–5

C
career 21, 23, 39, 70, 78,
  101, 107, 111, 117
cats 112, 113
Celtic deities 66–7, 90–1
change 17, 40–1, 42, 72–
  3, 77, 97, 100, 115
  embracing 21, 68,
    118–19
  guidance 70–1, 75, 77
  trickster attribute 124

charm 36, 62–3, 113
China 26, 72–3, 79, 92–3
cleansing 25, 65, 73,
  111, 118
clothing 47, 117
color 29, 47, 49, 60, 84,
  85, 114
comfort zone 43, 64, 65,
  105
communication 23, 42–3,
  50, 63, 68, 70, 78
confidence
  boosting 23, 38, 46–7,
    61, 62, 69, 117
  self-belief 67, 68–9, 75,
    76–7, 108–9, 113
courage 39, 46, 77
Coyote 6, 14–15, 124–5
creativity 15, 18–19, 63,
  66–7, 88, 93, 117, 122
creator gods 14, 20, 58,
  74, 76
Crow 6, 22–3

D
dance 63, 64, 87
decision-making 70–1,
  75, 77
deities 9, 58–9
  creator 20, 58, 74, 76
  Eris 68–9
  Eshu/Elegba/Legba 70–1
  Hermes 62–3
  Loki 60–1
  Lugh/Lugus 66–7
  Maui 74–5
  Nezha 72–3, 79
  Pan 64–5
  sky gods 15, 16, 76, 88
  Sun Wukong 26
  Tezcatlipoca 76–7
Denmark 50
destiny 15, 27, 37, 58
Discordia 68
divination 53, 71, 95
Dr Who 116–17
dragon 79, 92, 93
dreams 39, 53, 84, 94,
  96, 99, 114–15

E
emotional healing 19, 40,
  73, 90–1, 119
energy
  boosting 48, 63, 69,
    74–5, 111, 115
  healing 53
  negative 52, 74, 91
  positive 17, 113
  rituals 25, 65, 88–9,
    98–9, 116–17, 118–19
Eris 68–9
Eshu/Elegba/Legba 70–1
Europe
  Gwydion 88–9
  Hitar Petar 94–5
  Jack 84–5
  Loki 60–1
  the Pied Piper 46–7
  Puck 86–7
  Reynard the Fox 28–9
  Till Eulenspiegel 50–1

F
fairy tales 35, 46, 101
fate 58, 68
fear 35, 40, 64–5, 88,
  109, 125
figure of eight 47
flexibility 19, 29, 48,
  107, 112
food 26–7, 37, 52–3,
  67–8, 108–9
forests see trees
forgiveness 25, 53
foxes 28–9, 96
France 28
fun
  Bamapana 43
  Brer Rabbit 18
  deities 59, 64
  the Joker 110
  Monkey 27
  Pan 64, 65
  Puck 87
  Robin Hood 38
  Till Eulenspiegel 51
  Willy Wonka 121

G
Germany 35, 46, 50
goals 17, 25, 39, 96, 99
good fortune 36–7, 62,
  73, 84–5, 86–7,
    92–3, 107
Greece 62, 64–5, 68–9
Green Man 38
Gwydion 88–9

H
Hansel and Gretel 35
happiness 50–1, 69
hare 24, 25
healing 25, 53, 90
herbs 25, 52, 64–5, 94
Hermes 62–3, 66, 78
Herne the Hunter 38
Hero Twins, Mayan 98–9
Hitar Petar 94–5
home
  altar 66, 78, 79
  clearing 111
  harmonious 27, 48
  images in 25, 31, 91
  lost objects 48
  protection 29, 52
  the Saci 48–9
human tricksters 9, 34–5
  Appalachian Jack 36–7
  Bamapana 42–3
  the Mannegishi 44–5
  the Pied Piper 46–7
  Robin Hood 38–9
  the Saci 48–9
  Till Eulenspiegel 50–1
  Wakdjunkaga 52–3
  Whiskey Jack 40–1
humility 26, 52

I
imagination 18, 54, 71,
  79, 115, 122–3
inner self 23, 51, 115
insight 44–5, 70, 75
intuition 15, 44–5, 51,
  107, 113, 125
Ireland 66, 86, 90

126

J
Jack 84–5
  Appalachian Jack 36–7
  Jack of all trades 62, 66
  Jack Frost 118–19
  Jack Sparrow 6, 106–7
Japan, Kitsune 96–7
the Joker 51, 94–5, 110–11, 123
journal, keeping 97, 121
joy 27, 50, 86, 121, 125
justice 46

K
Kitsune 96–7

L
language 42, 43, 50, 95
laughter 51, 55, 64, 123
leadership 38
Legba 70–1
lessons from tricksters 83, 124
life
  determining future 27, 40, 53, 58, 70–1
  ebb and flow 15, 21, 124
  improving 54, 66, 68, 110, 118, 120–1
  transforming 42, 60, 72, 77, 115
little people 44–5
Loki 60–1
love 21, 90–1, 113, 119, 120
loved ones, lost 23
Lugh/Lugus 66–7

M
Manabozho 24–5
the Mannegishi 44–5
Maui 74–5
May Day 84
Mayan Hero Twins 98–9
mental agility 94–5, 112, 119
Mercury 62, 66
mistakes 25, 26, 52, 88–9
modern tricksters 9, 104–5
  Bugs Bunny 108–9
  Jack Sparrow 6, 106–7

Dr Who 116–17
  Jack Frost 118–19
  the Joker 110–11
  Peter Pan 114–15
  the Pink Panther 112–13
  Willy Wonka 120–1
Monkey 26–7
moon 18, 40, 98–9, 107, 118
movies/TV 106–23
music 47, 63, 64, 87

N
Native Americans
  Coyote 6, 14–15, 124–5
  Crow 6, 22–3
  Manabozho 24–5
  the Mannegishi 44–5
  Raven 6, 13, 14–15
  Wakdjunkaga 52–3
  Whiskey Jack 40–1
nature
  Gwydion 88, 89
  Lugh 67
  the Mannegishi 45
  Pan 64, 65
  Peter Pan 115
  Puck 86
  Robin Hood 38–9
  Whiskey Jack 41
Nezha 72–3, 79
Norse tales 60–1, 118
nutmeg 87

O
opportunities 43, 76, 110–11
owl 50, 51

P
Pan 64–5
past, letting go 27, 40, 72–3, 88, 118–19
perception 70, 71
personal magnetism
  Appalachian Jack 37
  Bugs Bunny 109
  Hermes 62
  Loki 61
  Pied Piper 46
  Pink Panther 113
  the Raven 21

Robin Hood 38
Peter Pan 114–15
Phouka 86
Pied Piper 46–7
Pink Panther 112–13
playing cards 51, 94, 110
Polynesian deity 74–5
Pooka 86
positive outlook 17, 29, 36, 66, 113, 117
problem-solving 17, 19, 29, 46, 49, 59, 75, 98–9
prosperity 84–5, 92–3, 107, 120
protection 28, 29, 48–9, 52, 63, 108
psychic skills 44, 45
Puck 86–7
Pwca 86

R
rabbits 18–19, 24, 25, 108–9
rats 46
Raven 6, 13, 20–1
rebelliousness 38, 52
rebirth 14, 34, 73
reinventing yourself 21, 27, 40–1, 72–3
relationships 17, 39, 70, 78, 90–1, 119
Reynard the Fox 28–9
Robin Goodfellow 86
Robin Hood 38–9
role of tricksters 5, 34–5, 36, 105

S
the Saci 48–9
self-belief 21, 23, 46, 68–9, 93, 108–9, 111
self-esteem 27, 38, 60, 95, 97
shape-shifters
  Bugs Bunny 108
  Dr Who 116
  Gwydion 88
  Kitsune 96
  Loki 60
  Manabozho 24
  Pied Piper 46

Puck 86
  the Saci 48
  Tezcatlipoca 76
skills 55, 66–7, 79, 97
sky gods 15, 16, 76, 88
snakes 22, 60, 68, 77
Sparrow, Capt Jack 6, 106–7
spider, Anansi 13, 16–17
spiritual guidance 70–1, 77, 125
spontaneity 42–3, 94, 97
stags 66
strength 38, 75, 77, 112
success 84–5, 92, 97, 107, 109, 120–1
sun 50, 74–5, 98–9
Sun Wukong 26
swans 90, 91

T
tarot cards 73, 110
Tezcatlipoca 76–7
Till Eulenspiegel 50–1
traditional tricksters 9, 82–3
  Aengus 90–1
  Bigmouth 92–3
  Gwydion 88–9
  Hitar Petar 94–5
  Jack 84–5
  Kitsune 96–7
  Mayan Hero Twins 98–9
  Puck 86–7
trees/forests 35, 38–9, 41, 64–5, 86, 88–9
truth 23, 46–7, 68, 69
types of trickster 8–9

W
Wakdjunkaga 52–3
Wales 86, 88
water 21, 44–5, 73, 75, 90, 107, 118
Whiskey Jack 40–1
wildlife 13, 30, 41
Willy Wonka 120–1
wind chimes 37, 114
Wisakeydjak 40–1
wisdom 27, 51
wish box 67, 96, 97

128

ACKNOWLEDGMENTS

I would like to say a big thank you to all the team at CICO Books for their help and hard work. In particular, I would like to thank Dawn Bates and Kristine Pidkameny, for being a joy to work with and for all their efforts in making the book a reality. I would like to thank the designer, Paul Tilby, and the illustrator, Qian Wu, for coming up with some lovely images that complement the text.